Lou Manfredini's
Bath Smarts

How to renovate and maintain the smallest— yet most essential— room in your home

Lou Manfredini's
Bath Smarts

How to renovate and maintain the smallest— yet most essential— room in your home

Lou Manfredini
with Curtis Rist

Ballantine Books
New York

A Ballantine Book
Published by The Random House Publishing Group

Copyright © 2004 by Lou Manfredini
Illustrations copyright © 2004 by Harry Trumbore

Ballantine and colophon are registered trademarks of Random House, Inc.

www.ballantinebooks.com

Library of Congress Control Number: 2004090456

ISBN 0-345-44990-8

Text design by Michaelis/Carpelis Design Assoc. Inc.

Manufactured in the United States of America

First Edition: May 2004

10 9 8 7 6 5 4 3 2 1

Acknowledgments

The book you're holding represents much of what I've learned about bathrooms in my years as a contractor. Yet like Sir Isaac Newton, who claimed to have had a clearer view than others because he had the advantage of "standing on the shoulders of giants," I've had it easy because I've worked with some amazing tradespeople over the years. True, I didn't actually hoist myself onto their shoulders. But I did make liberal use of their stepladders. They have taught me countless things about how to build and renovate homes.

I'd like to name a few of them here. First and foremost, my former partner and good friend Mike. Plumbers like Donny and Mo and Brice. Electricians like Jimmy and Bill, and heating guys such as Bill and Rick. Roofers like Brian and Jim, tile guys like Tom and Javier, drywall installers and plasterers like John and Louie. Concrete pourers and excavators like Guy and Jim—and who could forget Mark the painter?

On each project I worked on, this group came together like a team of players and worked to create beautiful bathrooms, no matter what the budget we had to work with. I learned so much from them, and I thank all of them and all the other countless tradespeople I've worked with who do this kind of work to perfection every single day.

What they know, I know—and now you'll soon know as you begin to read these pages.

Lou Manfredini

Contents

Introduction

A few years ago some acquaintances of mine named Mike and Diana had a problem, a great big problem the size of a nineteenth-century Colonial farmhouse. They had spent years restoring the outside of their white-clapboard house in New Jersey, and to great effect. Drivers on the road out front instinctively slowed down as they passed, to get a closer look. Luckily, they couldn't get *too* close a look, especially at the pair of bathrooms inside.

One of them was in "original condition," which is that wonderful real estate agent's euphemism for something that has been neglected for so many decades, it's suddenly fashionable again. Chic, perhaps, but this bathroom was far from inviting with its sagging floorboards, leaking toilet, and grim, cracked-plaster walls. It looked like something that would have been more at home in the Tower of London. In the upstairs bathroom, which they jokingly called the "good" bathroom, things were newer but no better. This room dated back to around 1968. It contained school bus–yellow ceramic tiles on the walls, the floors, and even the ceilings. All the fixtures, including the sink, the toilet, and the bathtub, matched, and the result was like some giant field of daffodils gone haywire. Besides this there were signs of serious structural trouble. Tiles had popped off sporadically here and there; and the entire shower wall, when pressed, jiggled and moved as if the supporting wall beneath it were made of Jell-O. "Got any suggestions?" Diana asked me tentatively. "Dynamite" crossed my mind briefly, but then a more optimistic thought prevailed. "Sure," I said. "But it's going to take a lot more than a new shower curtain and matching throw rug to pull this together."

Bathrooms are those house-defining spaces that people care about most. No matter how beautiful your home—whether it has the proverbial great "curb appeal," a wonderful cook's kitchen, or a fabulous layout and landscaping—these little rooms leave the ultimate lasting impression. After all, they are the most intimate places imaginable. Make a mental list of the obvious things that go on in a bathroom, then add some others. This is the place for the children's bath and toothbrushing ritual before bedtime, a place for the family to get ready for work and school with speed, and a place for a couple to unwind and relax in a hot tub at the end of the day. Where else in your home do you come in such close contact with the finished surfaces, and with so few clothes on, than in the bathroom? You can judge the rest of a house at arm's length—but that is hardly true of a bathroom.

This no doubt explains why we care so much about bathrooms, and why we're willing to spend so much money to get them right. According to a recent Harvard University study, Americans renovated an estimated 5 million bathrooms in the year 2001, and spent at least $5,000 on each one. This represents the low end of the scale, to be sure. In 2002, *Remodeling* magazine conducted a study of its own to show that Americans spent on the average of $10,000 for a mid-range remodel in 2002, which involved some of the following:

- a standard-sized tub with ceramic tile surrounding it
- a new toilet
- a new vanity, sink, and countertop
- a recessed medicine cabinet
- a ceramic tile floor

For upscale bathrooms, homeowners were willing to part with much more. For the same time period, *Remodeling* magazine reports the average price for a top-of-the-line bathroom ran to $23,500. This involved enlarging an existing 5-by-7-foot bathroom, and included some of the following upgrades:

- adding 30 square feet or more of windows and skylights
- relocating and replacing the tub with a custom shower containing top-of-the-line fittings
- relocating the toilet into a partitioned area, as well as adding a bidet
- adding a storage closet for linens and towels
- adding a humidistat-controlled exhaust system

Despite the obvious improvements in their day-to-day living, homeowners who renovate their bathrooms are also making a smart investment choice in terms of the resale value of their homes. Add a swimming pool, for instance, and you'll be lucky to recoup half the amount you spent when it comes time to sell your house. A kitchen gives a better return, with about 85 percent of your investment back if you sell within a few years. But the bathroom is off the charts, with a 117 percent increase in the value of your home. That means if you add a $20,000 bathroom today—and do it right—you could sell your house for $23,400 more tomorrow. That's not a bad dividend for some careful work, but the main benefit is that you get to live with it and enjoy it all the years you own your home.

Planning and renovating a bathroom can be a bewildering experience, a result of the huge number of choices now available. Some years ago, there was such a thing as a typical bathroom. This amounted to a 5-by-7-foot box that contained a sink, a toilet, and a bathtub. Today, by contrast, there is no such standard. You can tailor bathrooms for couples who want a little privacy and a place to relax at the end of the day, and for children, to maximize efficiency as they get ready in the morning. You can create bathrooms to meet the needs of people who are elderly or have special physical requirements. Then there are "half baths," or powder rooms, which in most homes contain the fancy soap and towels that often go unused, even by guests. Bathrooms can be built in basements to create a separate area for a relative, and they can be squeezed into unlikely spaces, such as under a staircase, when renovating an old house.

A bathroom renovation is likely to be the most complicated project you'll encounter as a homeowner. That's because there are so many factors involved. A bathroom's electricity, tiling, cabinetry, faucets, fixtures, plumbing, lighting, mirrors, medicine cabinets, and towel racks are all jammed into a space that sometimes extends no more than 35 little square feet. In some ways it resembles those portraits-in-miniature, in which the artists work with paintbrushes containing a single hair or two, and this is similar to the task awaiting anyone working on a bathroom. There's simply no room to maneuver, and no room for error. Plus, the space quickly becomes crowded with workers, including the electrician, the plumber, the carpenter, and the mason. Managing a crew like this, as well as coming up with the correct order in which to do things, takes all the skill of an air traffic controller at JFK airport the day before Thanksgiving. Even simple mistakes can lead to delays and cost overruns, and can prevent you from creating the bathroom of your dreams.

I can't make the challenge simply go away, but I can make the process of renovating a bathroom more manageable. I can help you create a realistic design, develop a budget that works, and show you choices to make that will suit the way you and your family live. Of course, this is going to be a difficult journey—not least of all because you have to find a new place to shower for the duration of the project—but the process will be worth it. You'll end up with a bathroom that looks great, is a joy to live with, and adds real value to your home.

My friends Mike and Diana discovered this in the course of rebuilding their two bathrooms. Gone were the school bus–yellow tiles and the squishy floorboards, and in their place went surfaces and fixtures that not only look good but will last for decades. Although no one slows down outside just to catch a glimpse of one of their bathrooms through the windows, the rebuilt rooms help make their home feel every bit as grand on the inside as it is on the outside.

The same can be true of your home, no matter what the size of your budget or your bathroom.

Lou Manfredini's
Bath Smarts

How to renovate and
maintain the smallest—
yet most essential—
room in your home

chapter ONE

So What's the Plan?

Designing and renovating a bathroom requires a grand strategy; here's how to devise it.

Let me tell you about the last bathroom I ever remodeled in which I quoted a fixed price up front.

The project involved a beautiful stucco house with a red-tiled roof, owned by a colleague of my wife. My partner Mike and I had built a screened-in porch for her the year before, and the homeowner was so pleased with our work, she called us back to redo her bathroom. No problem for us; after all, we like to think of ourselves as full-service renovators. As with all bathrooms we had worked on, we knew this one would involve quite a number of contractors from various trades, from plumbers to electricians, so we diligently figured this in to our contract price of $18,500. Although there was nothing particularly fancy about this project, it did involve stripping the old bathroom down to the studs and starting over, including new fixtures, new tile floors and wainscoting, and even a new window.

I had to admit, the bathroom came out like a dream. We even tended to the small details, such as pulling out the large cast-iron radiator that was taking up space and replacing it with cast-iron baseboard heat, which made the room appear bigger. The homeowner was thrilled, so

Color My World

In the old days, every bathroom fixture was white, from the sink and the tub to the toilet. Something happened in the middle of the twentieth century to change that, and the fuchsia sinks, midnight blue toilets, and black bathtubs are here to remind us that versatility in color does not always guarantee good taste.

The average homeowner tends to be somewhat fearful of color, and considering all the pitfalls that await those willing to make "bold choices," I think that's a good thing. While I don't want to begrudge anyone from being creative with color, I do want to offer some words in defense of restraint. First, it's easy to change the colors of walls, and of accents such as towels and floor mats. If you're going to be bold, these are the places to start. That way, when you change your mind, you can alter them without having to renovate the entire bathroom. But when choosing colors for tubs, sinks, and toilets, as well as ceramic or natural stone tiles, I'd take it easy. Choose colors and materials that allow you the most wide-ranging ability to decorate. This means "subtle" with a capital S. Stick to white or almond for fixtures, beige or off-white for tiles, and ordinary chrome or brass for faucets. As with a pot of Texas chili, it's easy to spice things up with a few additions—but you can never spice things down without starting from scratch.

Mike and I packed up our tools and headed home. It wasn't until we started writing checks to pay all those various contractors that we realized we had a problem. We paid the electrician, the plumber, and the tile setter, a nice guy named Phil who did terrific work. Then we discovered that the $18,500 bathroom we had just installed had actually cost $26,300—and that Mike and I would be paying the difference. It was then that I formulated my cardinal rule, which holds true to this day: You will exceed your budget on a bathroom renovation, no matter what.

Bathroom design is one of the trickiest of all, and not just because the budget is so hard to control. Nowhere else in the house is so much going on in so little square footage—from sinks and toilets to tubs and showers, and places to store and dry towels and clothes. Even the dirty laundry heaps up in here. Think for a moment of what else the bathroom holds: magazines and books to peruse, in what has become the twenty-first-century "library"; cosmetics and colognes; mirrors, medicine cabinets, wastepaper baskets; spare linens and towels. This room is part attic, part utility room, and all under intensive use. In addition, homeowners now look to the bathroom in the master suite as a place to unwind from the stresses of the day, as if the deteriorated conditions found in the average bathroom wouldn't *compound* the stresses of the day. On top of it, this is the harshest environment outside the Amazon jungle: It's subjected to daily dousings from steamy water, which makes the entire room humid and damp. Yet we all want everything to feel fresh and look pristine.

How do you get that? By going beyond the basics of decorating to focus on the underlying systems and structure that make a bathroom durable. To create a bathroom that feels fresh, that soothes the senses, and that maintains household harmony by providing a place that family members can use efficiently and in close proximity, you have to think about it from top to bottom and then again from bottom to top. This doesn't mean you have to spend a fortune for a full renovation to improve conditions, but you do have to think beyond décor to get to the vital organs of this most vexing of rooms.

Let's begin our tour of bathroom renovation by focusing on design basics before we work through the major aspects of renovation in the chapters that follow.

Designed to Please

Bathing has a long and rather weird history. Back in the days of the ancient Greeks, in the city of Sparta, the idea for a bath was decidedly, well, Spartan. A warrior would stand in a small basin and have his slave douse him with cold water (think Kirk Douglas). We've evolved from that, fortunately—beginning with the wise decision to bring the bathing ritual indoors and add hot water to it. The first bathrooms became popular in the mid-1800s, and helped give Millard Fillmore a claim to fame. His accomplishments as president may be forgettable, but he deserves special credit as the first one to have a bathtub in the White House. Everyone else slowly followed into the twentieth century, but it wasn't until the post–World War II building craze that bathrooms as we know them— plentiful, uniform, and convenient—began to appear in houses.

If there's any part of a home that's completely personal and a perfect canvas for a homeowner to express his or her individuality, it's the bathroom. For some, it's simply a basic necessity, not a luxury. I constantly hear people asking questions such as, "I'm tired of cleaning the old grout, what can I do to fix it?" These are people who do not want to hear about

The Rule of Fives

There are many choices for materials and fixtures in a bathroom—too many, in fact. This often leads to an inability to actually make selections. To combat this, follow my simple rule of fives. As you're searching for things—toilets, for instance—keep looking until you find five that would satisfy you, and then call a halt to the process. Force yourself to make your final choice based on the five you've narrowed down, and then move on to the next item. Unless you manage the process this way, you'll never get your bathroom started, let alone finished, because you'll become so mired in all the choices that exist.

what shade of marble was recently discovered in a mine in Brazil this year that would be perfect in a lavish master bathroom suite. Instead, they want to know the basics about making a small room look and work better. Regardless of the goal, however, the essential rules of bathroom design are the same, whether it's a small room that needs updating, or a large one that involves a major renovation. Understanding what goes on in this room will help you make efficient use of your dollars, whether you have $1,000 or $100,000 to spend.

Per square foot, a bathroom has more equipment than any other room in the house. It is pricey acreage, and every inch counts. At the same time, bathrooms today are being asked to do more: accommodate more people, give them more privacy, provide generous storage, and include luxury amenities such as steam showers and whirlpools. Squeezing it all in is no easy task: It's like piecing together a puzzle, and sometimes you have to draw it a hundred times to get everything to fit. But whether the puzzle is a compact powder room, a kid-friendly family bath, or a spa-style master retreat, the approach to solving it always starts the same way. First, consider who will be using the space. Next, think about the number and style of fixtures you would like to incorporate in the plan. And finally, work out where those fixtures can be placed.

Let's walk through the major types of bathrooms to find the plan that suits you best.

The Half Bath

My friends Mike and Judy just remodeled their kitchen, and the result is beautiful. But what catches everyone's attention is the new powder room. True, it's as tiny as anything could be, but instead of an ordinary sink, they have a ceramic bowl custom-made by an artisan. The water spills out into a bowl that is blue, with silver flecks, and the effect is mesmerizing. Whenever we visit them, my four-year-old daughter inevitably disappears. I know right where to find her, however. She'll be standing in the powder room, watching the water splash into the bowl she loves.

Most people try to spruce up their powder room by adding tiny little hand towels and oddly shaped balls of soap to show off to their guests. A better approach, I think, is to use the room as a showcase for some

Location, Location, Location

Location is important in choosing a site for a powder room because privacy is so essential. You don't want to access it directly from the living room, the dining room, the family room, or even the kitchen. Instead, do everything you can to tuck it into an alcove off a hallway.

clever piece of design—such as my friends' sink, or some other architectural detail. Small and intimate, this is a room that can have enormous appeal. Yet with only two fixtures—the sink and the toilet—it is a room that practically designs itself. Minimum dimensions are amazingly compact: You can fit a sink and a toilet into less than 20 square feet and still satisfy the prying eyes of the local building inspector. If space is tight, you can have a small sink attached directly to the wall, rather than a larger pedestal sink. You can

A Tired Theme

No matter how cute the idea may seem at first, I would caution against adding themed bathrooms for children, whether the theme is Snow White or the Chicago Cubs. These may look great for a year, but very quickly they'll become as dated and annoying as Barney the purple dinosaur. A better approach is this: If you want to have a theme for a bathroom, limit it to wallpaper and accessories such as towels and floor mats rather than structural things such as tiles and cabinets. The wallpaper can easily be changed as your family develops other tastes; the tiles and fixtures cannot.

also save space by using a round, rather than elongated, toilet.

A half bath doesn't need much in the way of storage or counter-tops, since no one is likely to set up camp there for long. There are some practical considerations, however, starting with the entrance. If possible, the door should swing *into* the room rather than out, even though that will eat up floor space. A door requires at least its own width in cleared floor space in order for it to swing open, and additional room to maneuver it so that someone inside the bathroom can shut the door without having to stand on the toilet to clear some space. Don't laugh; I have seen situations where this is the case. An in-swinging door also avoids the problem of where to "store" the open door, rather than having it dangle open and take up space in another room or hallway. If the space is too small for an in-swinging door, add

Five Rules of Bathroom Renovation

Much of what I know about houses I learned the hard way—that is, through trial and error, with the emphasis on error. To save you disappointments and cost overruns, here are five things to keep in mind while designing and renovating your bathroom:

1. Rather than relying on what a contractor or designer tells you, spend time gathering your own information, on the Internet and from books, magazines, and TV, to get a feel for what you can do. The stronger your opinions, the more likely you'll get the results you want.

2. To come up with a realistic budget, begin by pricing everything at retail, even if you know you will eventually get some things at a discount. Inevitably, we choose pricier items as the project goes along, but this will be compensated by the bargains and discounts found in other areas. The result will be a budget that's realistic rather than a fantasy.

3. Make sure you go far enough with the renovation. A renovation is a difficult project that will tie up the household for weeks, if not months. Rather than save some aspect, such as a new tub or shower, of the bathroom for later, it's better to get it all done at once.

4. Come up with a realistic timetable for how long the project will take. This is especially necessary if you'll be doing the work yourself, but is also essential if you'll be working with a contractor. As a rule of thumb, double the time you think it will take, and then add two extra days. This will be a good approximation of the completion date.

5. Check your contractor's references. Ask to see a portfolio of the projects he has worked on, and ask to visit the bathrooms he has built. Happy customers are more than eager to show off their new bathrooms, so this should hardly be seen as an imposition. They can give you great insight into what the contractor is like to work with.

a sliding-pocket door instead, which allows you to keep the door open without blocking the hallway.

The Family Bath

The family bath is a serious workspace. It's got at least three fixtures, including the toilet, sink, and combination bathtub/shower, and is also the central depository for toothbrushes, towels, medicine, and all kinds of grooming gear. Whereas no homeowner wants to share the master bathroom with the rest of the household, the opposite is true for other bathrooms—particularly those for children. Since bathrooms rank as expensive renovations, creating one to serve two or more family members can offer significant savings. The key to making a shared bathroom work lies in what architects call compartmentalization. Rather than having a single room filled with a tub, sink, and toilet, the fixtures in a shared bathroom should be in separate places to make it possible for someone to use the sink while someone else is using the toilet. While you're at it, adding two sinks and two areas for brushing teeth and grooming will make the mornings move along much more quickly when children are involved.

At the same time, a separate toilet stall (often called a water closet, or a WC) can open up a room to more than one user at a time without sacrificing privacy. Such a space should be at least 36 inches wide and 66 inches deep for maximum comfort. Another option is a stall with half-height walls, which feels less cramped, lets in more light, and eliminates door-swing issues. Bathing is the last piece of the puzzle. Remember that regardless of size, a bathtub needs at least a 12-inch clearance from any adjacent fixture and 36 inches of cleared floor space for someone to get in and out easily. If you're looking to conserve floor space, a shower stall takes up about half the area of a tub, although you'll have to account for door swing if you're not satisfied with a shower curtain. If you opt for a shower, choose a stall that is at least 36 inches square; anything smaller will feel claustrophobic.

Big, Bigger, Biggest

If there's one certainty in life, it's this: Bathrooms are getting bigger—an average of 22 percent larger than bathrooms that were built two decades ago. If you're building a new house, it's easy enough to find space for a larger bathroom. But if you're renovating an existing bathroom, the extra space comes at a premium.

Over the years I've become adept at squeezing a few extra square feet from odd locations. Often, there is a closet adjacent to the other side of a wall, and incorporating it into the bathroom is a simple project. And sometimes I have found areas, which are called chases, that are hollow areas in the wall used to carry plumbing, electrical, or heating systems. These areas are often sized far larger than they need to be, or were designed for equipment that is no longer in use, and can easily be annexed into the new bathroom. It might be exactly the additional space you need to add a small linen closet, a larger tub, or a steam shower.

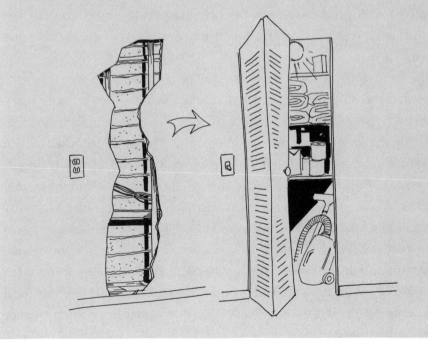

One of the things you need to do in a family-friendly bath is make sure your children can actually reach the sink. In general, I'm a big fan of vanity sinks that are installed at regular kitchen countertop height, of about 32 inches, but that's because I'm 6 foot 3 and my wife, Mary Beth, is over 5 foot 10. Our kids are not that tall, but someday they will be. Rather than add lower sinks and counters for them, I've solved the problem a different way. For my youngest daughter, Mallory, I built a solid bench that sits firmly on the floor without wiggling. When she wants to brush her teeth, she slides it out from beneath the sink and stands on it. This way, everyone else in the family can use the sink, too, without feeling like they are living in Munchkinland.

One other factor to consider with a family bath is noise. Put a bathroom between two bedrooms and someone will always be waking up someone else when they use it. A solution to this is to use clothes closets as sound barriers to separate the bedroom from the bathroom. This should help muffle the din and allow everyone a peaceful night.

The Master Bath

One place homeowners tend to be willing to spend more renovation dollars than anywhere else in the house is a master bathroom. This is the main domain, after all, the place where the masters of the house start each morning and end each evening.

A half century ago, the average household would have been well served by a single, 5-by-7-foot bathroom. Functional? Surely it is, but it's not in keeping with today's families. No longer are bathrooms basic, functional rooms—especially those in the master suite. Now they include chairs or chaises for lounging and reading, dressing areas adjacent to walk-in closets, and, in some cases, a TV and a stereo system. We're seeing things added to bathrooms that Mom and Dad in the '50s and '60s never dreamed of: dressing rooms, walk-in closets, steam showers, soaking tubs, even refrigerators. This is no longer a room where you take a bath or a shower and run. It's a room in which to

A Case for Vinyl

Ordinarily I like windows made of wood, but in a bathroom these can be impractical because of the constant humidity. A better choice for this room is high-quality windows made of vinyl. They'll look great and be able to stand up to years of use.

relax, where all kinds of activities can take place, from reading books to making phone calls.

A family bathroom focuses on utility, but a master bathroom is about comfort and relaxation. A master bath is no longer a compartment. It's really more like another room in your house. And, like a room, it requires space: at least 80 square feet for a toilet, sink, shower, and an extravagance such as a spa and/or whirlpool. Even in a large space, the layout is very important. A separate shower is essential for quick washups on busy mornings; a tub becomes a beautiful focal point for the room; and two sinks are a must, and should be separated by at least 3 feet so that you don't bump elbows with your mate. Also, the mirror behind the sink should be somewhat larger than life—the bigger the better, particularly if two people are going to be jockeying to use it. The most critical placement of all, however, is the toilet's. To be honest, it's not at all pleasant to sit on one that faces the center of an enormous space; you feel too exposed. It's better to create privacy by tucking the toilet into an alcove—or, better still, in a small room with a door. Storage becomes crucial as well, to help organize linens and towels, as well as dirty laundry.

As the master bathroom expands in size, so does the need for natural light. A window or two makes a bathroom more pleasant to be in and, more importantly, helps ventilate moisture and odors. The placement of the bathtub can help in this regard. Because the tub doesn't occupy much upper-wall space, it can be used as an opportunity to add windows, bring in natural light, improve ventilation, and allow a glimpse of any views—which, you hope, will be of something other than the neighbors.

The ABCs of Universal Design

Some years ago I worked on a large bathroom for a man and his wife who were both confined to wheelchairs. The result was no ordinary 5-by-7-foot bathroom, to be sure. It had to be large enough for both of them to maneuver around in it at the same time, and while they did need assistance with some things such as bathing, they wanted to be able to handle other aspects by themselves—such as brushing their teeth. This was accomplished by elevating the sinks high enough so that they could wheel right up to them. In addition, the pipes below were pitched so they wouldn't interfere with the wheelchairs, and we even padded them in case anyone bumped into them with their knees. The result was surprisingly inviting: It was convenient for the home-owners, and it had great style. It gave them pride in their home *and* complemented their lifestyle—which should be the goals of any bathroom, no matter what.

A "universal bathroom," as this one is called, is one that is designed to meet the needs of people of all "ages, sizes, and abilities," according to the American Association of Retired Persons (AARP), but the term has come to refer also to bathrooms that conform to a set of standards established by the Americans with Disabilities Act (ADA). Prescribed measurements and clear-

Getting a Grip

Did you ever see a three-year-old try to turn a doorknob? He or she can't, and neither can many other people. Instead of a knob, installing a door handle or lever is a better choice. They're easy for everyone to use, even when one's hands are full, and they cost only a dollar or two more than a knob.

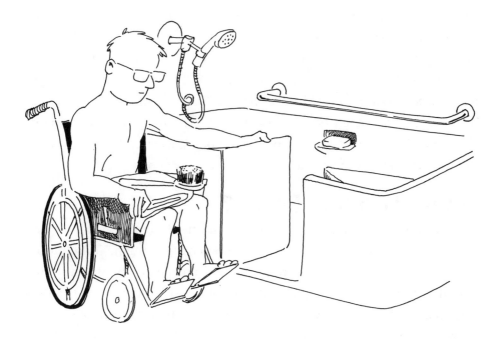

ances govern every aspect of the room's layout and fittings in order to accommodate a person using a wheelchair, the largest piece of equipment someone with a disability might require. This includes having the 5-foot diameter that the ADA requires for a wheelchair to turn.

Other requirements include having a barrier-free, roll-in shower, which in this case turned the entire room into a shower, with no curb to block the passage of the wheelchair. For more details about these requirements, check the AARP's Web site at www.aarp.org. There are some additional features that can make bathrooms easier, though these are not specifically spelled out by the ADA. You should always use nonslip tiles, such as unglazed porcelain, to cover the floor, rather than shiny materials such as polished marble. The tiles should be no larger than 4 inches square, and I even prefer tiny mosaic tiles that measure about half an inch on each side. These allow more grout per square foot, which is great for traction; also, the mosaics tend to follow the contour of the floor better, and thus make for a more maneuverable surface.

The goal in designing a universal bathroom is to make it a beautiful room without calling attention to its purpose. The best thing about a universal bath is that it works for everybody. Because of the lower position of its fixtures, children will feel comfortable there, as will older people with no particular physical disabilities. Making everybody comfortable is what good design is all about.

Where Should I Begin?

Considering the variety of bathrooms, it should come as no surprise that there are countless approaches to renovating them. To help guide you, I've come up with a strategy for what projects you might undertake if you had various budgets to spend—including $350, $1,000, $5,000, and, finally, no limit whatsoever. Let's begin on the low end of the spectrum.

Go to any home center and you'll find a huge number of products that you can use to give your bathroom a low-cost makeover. In one weekend you can literally change the way everything looks. Let's start with a gallon of paint and some primer. If you have $50 and a few hours, you can make a huge cosmetic difference in the room. First, wash the walls, then prime them and next coat them with paint containing an eggshell satin finish for easier cleaning. Now comes the hardware. Shop for a new faucet. A good-quality, single-lever faucet, made with solid brass construction inside, will cost from $50 to $100. Installing this is actually a do-it-yourself job, which should spare you the plumber's fee. A new showerhead might run anywhere from $60 to $100, and is just as easy to install. I like the new spa-style of showerhead, which is about 6 inches in diameter and has a curve in it that actually raises the height of the showerhead. While you're pushing the shopping cart, pick up a new shower curtain and new shower rings, which will probably run you another $50. If you want, you can also add new towel bars, towel rings, and toilet-paper holder, for probably $50. That's it; you've just remade the bathroom for $350 or under. Although this wouldn't change the underlying structure of a bathroom, it would spice things up. And it's the perfect cost-effective approach if you live in an apartment or rental home.

Befriending a Bathroom Designer

Let's face it: Not all of us are comfortable with the thought of working with someone who bills himself or herself as an interior decorator. Perhaps it's our sense that they'll charge us twice what it would cost to do the job ourselves. Or that we'll end up with a bathroom decorated in Ming vases and Louis XIV divans, when all we wanted was a wastepaper basket and a comfy wicker chair. I, however, am living proof that designers can offer great support, especially when it comes to a project that needs as much fine-tuning and micromanagement as a bathroom. I used an interior designer in my own house, and the result is far better than I could ever have produced on my own.

A good designer will ask you questions that move the planning process way beyond décor. They'll ask if you and your spouse are a working couple and, if so, if you get up at the same time and use the bathroom together. They'll want to find out if there's a need for a walk-in closet adjacent to the bathroom, and will help you determine whether that $10,000 steam shower you think you crave is worthwhile or a wasted extravagance. To get the most from a designer, be prepared to tell him or her everything personal about how you use this vital space in your house. A designer has an understanding of what works, based on years of experience. They'll also advise you on obscure products that most contractors probably won't know about—such as the perfect, curved 14-inch vanity that would fit into a nook in the room.

Now, if you're in the $1,000 range, you'll do everything I just mentioned as well as some other more intensive projects. For starters, you can add a new integrated sink and countertop for the vanity, which will probably cost about $100. A new toilet will most likely be in order, for another $150, and you may even be able to put down some simple 4-by-4-inch ceramic tiles on the floor. This would probably cost another $200. You would be able to add a new medicine cabinet for another $100, and would probably have enough left over to spring for a new light fixture. You could install some of these things yourself, but even with help from a plumber and an electrician, or even a tile setter, the labor costs would not exceed a few hundred dollars. The result would be that every surface would have a fresh new look.

Beyond this, you can accomplish a rather extensive renovation for under $5,000, and literally transform every surface in the bathroom. To do this, you would include everything I mentioned in the $1,000 renovation. Then you would tackle the final surfaces that I did not mention: the bathtub or shower stall. For about $100, you could buy new faucets to freshen things up. But, more important, you can actually have a high-quality acrylic surround set in place over an existing tub or shower. I will go into this process in more detail in Chapter 5, but the result is a tub and shower that look like new for the bargain cost of about $2,500. While you're at it, you'll want to add a new exhaust fan to help clear away moisture, and you may want a shower door rather than a shower curtain. You can also replace the entire vanity cabinet rather than just the countertop. This would totally revamp an existing bathroom without the expense and angst of a gut rehab.

Let's prepare now for the ultimate bathroom. Although this falls into the "over $5,000" category, in reality there is no limit to how much this can cost, whether it is $10,000, $15,000, or even $50,000 and more. By definition, projects of this scope involve a gut renovation. In addition, they also frequently involve moving the plumbing and electrical fixtures to new locations, rather than leaving them where they were in the old bathroom. An architect or experienced contractor is crucial to the success of a project this big, because there are too many possibilities for costly mistakes. Also, if you're going to start moving the plumbing and electrical wiring around, you will need an expert to be involved in order to get whatever building permits you may need, as well as to secure approvals from co-op or condo boards if the renovations involve an apartment. Most cities and towns require you to submit something called a riser diagram for the plumbing, which details where the waste and vent lines will go—something I will describe in greater detail in Chapter 3. As a dividend for the municipality, this also gives them a chance to raise your tax assessment based on the new bathroom, but there is little you can do about this. A new bathroom will increase the value of your home, both for better and for worse.

Once the basic plumbing, wiring, and structural renovations are made, the new bathroom is ready to go. With an empty space, you'll be free to choose any type of tub, shower, tiles, sinks, and vanity cabinets. Add to this the lighting, ventilation, and painting, and the minimum cost, from my experience, will be somewhere between $15,000 and $20,000. It's at this point that many homeowners become scared, and even ponder the wisdom of returning to the outhouse. In most cases, the bathroom is just as expensive as the kitchen, even though it is so much smaller. That is

Gut Renovation versus Simple Makeover

How do you know when it's time to say good-bye to your old bathroom rather than simply try to spruce it up? If you've got loose tiles, squishy walls or floors, nonworking fixtures, serious mold and mildew, or cramped and uncomfortable surroundings, it's time to go for the big overhaul.

Demolition for All

We're a country of do-it-yourselfers, or at least do-it-yourself wannabes. In reality, we seldom have the time to learn to do correctly a task such as carpentry or tiling, much as we would want to save the money. The exception to this is demolition. If ever there is a skill that needs no finesse—other than the ability to swing a sledgehammer and work a crowbar—this is it. It also marks the best way for homeowners to get involved and save money on their bathroom renovation.

During a gut renovation of a bathroom, everything has to go: the walls, the flooring, the fixtures—even that stack of *Saturday Evening Post*s from 1952. This renovation involves removing toilets, disassembling vanity sinks, loosening countertops and cabinets, tearing off tiles from walls, ripping up flooring, and getting rid of plaster. Sounds easy? Not really. It's messy, sweaty work, and is best accomplished with a group of friends, as long as you remember to put a lasagna in the oven first, to offer as a reward for the finished job. Before you begin, make sure you talk with the contractor, who will see to it that water pipes are shut off, electrical wires are disconnected, and rags are stuffed into the open sewer line connections to stop gases from venting. This will be a difficult task, but you could easily save $1,500 off the cost of renovating a medium-sized bathroom.

because the work of so many different trades is represented, even if served up in tinier portions. The good news is that if you renovate a bathroom and do it well, it will probably last a generation—with some occasional cosmetic fine-tuning along the way.

To make sure you get a bathroom that lasts, however, let's move on to the most important aspect of creating a bathroom that will last—which is how to manage its climate.

chapter TWO

Climate Control
What's the biggest challenge in creating a beautiful bathroom? Managing dampness and humidity.

I have an acquaintance named Sam who wanted to redo his bathroom himself. This is a great idea, as long as you know what you're doing—which, unfortunately, Sam did not.

The house dated from 1910, with tall ceilings and beautiful pointed gables. He was determined to make it a nice place, and so he headed for the home improvement center for everything he needed, including a new toilet and sink, a bathtub, and tiles. He worked nights after work and every weekend installing things, and studied how-to guides and instruction manuals to do it all himself. When it was completed he was proud of his work, as was his family. But it wasn't to last.

For one thing, the bathroom was cold in the winter, so stepping on the tiles would make everyone shriek, as would sitting on the toilet itself. A trip to the bathroom is supposed to be a comfortable experience, not one that recalls Admiral Perry's expedition to the North Pole. Annoying as this was, the moisture proved far worse. Nothing ever seemed to dry out in the windowless room, and Sam would have to prop open the door and put a fan on to air things out. Towels stayed damp for days on end, and a perennial fog clung to the mirrors whenever anyone got out of the shower. Over time things began to smell damp, then foul, and within a couple of years, dark patches of mold began to form in the corners. "I did everything right, followed every direction, and this is the bathroom I end up with," Sam said in disgust. "It's just as bad as the one I ripped out."

This is often the case, especially with do-it-yourself jobs that neglect a few key points. Bathrooms are unique in the house with respect to climate, because they contain so much moisture. Think of an Amazon rain jungle—or, better yet, those automatic sprayers in the produce aisle at your local supermarket—and you will have a good idea of what is going on in the bathroom. In the rush to put on finishes, great tiles, and towel racks and install new toilets and bathtubs, this is sometimes a factor that gets left out. It's as if we imagine the bathroom will somehow be able to cope all by itself with the abuse heaped upon it. This is absolutely wrong. Without careful ventilation, a bathroom will turn into a peeling, cracking, nasty-looking mold-and-mildew magnet in no time. People so often want to spend their renovation dollars on the finished parts they can see rather than on the underlying systems that make a bathroom comfortable. This is self-defeating because these hidden aspects cannot be overlooked if the goal is to create a comfortable bathroom that lasts.

Let's focus on moisture, then move on to other elements of comfort that you have to consider at the beginning of a bathroom renovation. Although you may not be spending your money where you thought you would, the results will be more than worth it.

Good-bye, Greenhouse Effect

What's the number one enemy in the quest to create a great bathroom? No, not teenagers, who tend to monopolize this space. And no, not what we can politely refer to as "odors." The answer is moisture. In normal operation, the average bathroom becomes as steamy as a greenhouse.

True, there are splashes that happen around the sinks and baths, but these are minor compared to a different kind of threat. I am talking about moisture that erupts in plumes when the hot water is turned on. It hangs

in the air and creates a dampness that withers all but the best-designed bathrooms. The amount of humidity generated by taking showers and baths is monumental. Studies show that the average family of four creates four gallons of moisture a day just by living in their home, and a whopping two-thirds of that comes from bathing. With a volume this large, you can't remedy things simply by clucking at family members to take shorter showers, or by trying to get them to be neater when toweling off. Instead, you need to have systems designed and installed that remove humidity from the room itself. This is known as ventilation, and in the bathroom it should come in two forms: mechanical and natural. Let's first take a look at natural ventilation.

Although it may sound complicated, natural ventilation refers to nothing more than an open window. Yet as obvious as the need for this should be, it is often overlooked. It is certainly possible to live with a bathroom that does not have a window; in fact, in the past, I have built these many times myself. But a windowless expanse will make the challenge of

Windowless Ventilation

If it's not possible to add a window to a bathroom to draw in fresh air, an alternative solution exists—in the form of a fresh-air intake. This is simply a vent cut through the wall to the exterior that contains a register that can be opened and closed on the inside. On the outside, it is covered with a duct similar to the ones that ventilate a clothes dryer. When you want fresh air, just open the register. At about $100, this is much cheaper than installing a window, and doesn't interfere as much with space requirements or with the way a home looks from the exterior.

creating a moisture-free bathroom that much more difficult, especially in warm months. In addition to filling a bathroom with light, the window provides the most effective form of ventilation to help keep your bathroom fresh. Anytime you have the opportunity to add some type of window, no matter how small or oddly placed, grab it.

It's possible to put a window anywhere in a bathroom, but my favorite

In Praise of Vinyl

Like many people, I'm a fan of natural materials, especially with regard to windows. To paraphrase Patrick Henry, give me wood, or give me death! The exception to this, however, is in a bathroom window. An all-wood window here might satisfy purists wanting to capture the old-fashioned integrity of a house, but it hardly makes practical sense, especially if it's located in the shower area. After a year or two of being splashed with water, it simply won't hold up. That's why, for this area, my window of choice is an all-vinyl one.

Now, mention the words "vinyl windows" and a cheesy image comes to mind of something that costs $50 at a home center and has all the structural integrity of a plastic bag. This is not what I am talking about. I am talking about vinyl windows made by reputable window manufacturers. These are high-quality vinyl windows that might cost $300 to $400, which does not include the cost of installation.

What's perfect about a window such as this in a bathroom is its resiliency. You can splash it with water and the water will simply drip off. In fact, you could hose it down daily and in a decade it would still perform as well as the day it was installed. And the best
part is this: It will
never rot; and since
it isn't painted, you
won't have to worry
about any peeling
from all the bath-
room humidity.

location is directly in the shower and tub area. Commonly seen in older homes, these windows are wooden, which means they have a tendency to weather their daily dousings badly. Old wooden windows will inevitably rot in these locations, and even newer wooden windows can have difficulty holding a coat of paint as a result of all the moisture. Ordinarily I love all-wood windows—or those that are wood on the inside and clad with maintenance-free vinyl or aluminum on the out-side—but this is one place where I make a major exception. When installed directly in the shower or tub area, I recommend a high-quality pure vinyl window. Since it's vinyl, it will be impervious to the water; in fact, you can aim the showerhead directly at it and no harm will come to it. The shower surround, whether it is made of tile or an acrylic liner

Fawning over Awnings

When it comes to choosing the best type of window for a bathroom, the choice is obvious: an awning window. This is similar to a casement window that cranks open, except it is hinged on the top, and tilts open more like a flap. To me, an awning window is the slam-dunk solution for providing a bathroom with natural ventilation.

What makes an awning window great for a bathroom? It can stay open in the rain, and will shed water off the top of it and away from the house rather than allow water to pour into the bath-room. In a driving rain, some water might penetrate the open window, but that's okay—this is a bathroom. And if the window is located in a shower area, a little extra water splashing in will hardly be noticed amid the daily spray.

Finding a Home for a Window

If you have a windowless bathroom and you're doing only a minor renovation, the chances are you're stuck with it. But if you're doing an extensive renovation, then I believe you should never settle for a bathroom without a window.

In the rush to renovate my own home a few years ago, I hastily designed a bathroom adjacent to my eldest son's room, which had no windows. While I managed to feel sort of proud that I had squeezed a 6-by-6-foot bathroom out of what had been nothing but a closet, my sister-in-law Nora told me she didn't like it at all. The reason: It didn't have a window. I pointed out that it *did* have an exhaust fan, but she still didn't go for it. Clearly, she had been listening to me expound about such things for too many years, and would not be easily convinced. Instead, she took a look at the blueprints and suggested a simple fix that involved putting the bathroom on the outside wall, and adding a window.

I slid the bathroom down 6 feet closer to the outer wall and cut a hole in the outside wall to add a small awning window. This might have cost me all of about $400 in materials. The result is a gem of a bathroom that not only has adequate ventilation in the summer months, it also catches the morning light. Best of all, it bears absolutely no resemblance to the closet that spawned it.

(which I will discuss in Chapter 5), is then cut so that it abuts the window, and the gap between the two surfaces caulked to form a watertight joint.

That will take care of the window, but what about the windowsill? Again, in most homes—new as well as old—these are wood, since they form part of the trim installed by a carpenter. Yet for the same reasons, wood is a terrible choice in this location. A classier choice for a windowsill—and one that will also hold up to an infinite amount of water—is a piece of cut stone, such as marble or granite. This sounds like a luxury, but it's actually one of those little accents that only seems extravagant. In reality, it is as practical as anything could be. We're used to seeing stone countertops that cost thousands of dollars. But if you go to a

A Frosty Reception

When installing a window in a bathroom, use opaque or frosted glass for privacy. This will screen you from the prying eyes of neighbors, let in light, and free you from having to add a blind or drapes, which are difficult to maintain in the humidity of a bathroom. In a bathroom, an awning window works best—the type that cranks open from the bottom.

Whereas a traditional double-hung window opens wide to the world, an awning window opens just a crack, which limits the line of sight into the bathroom.

stonecutting yard, they will have a mountain of scraps they will be more than willing to let you rummage through, to find some they can then fabricate into a windowsill. First, however, make sure your carpenter provides you with the dimensions you need—or, better yet, makes you a life-sized sketch called a template that can serve as a pattern for the cut. When the stone windowsill is installed, have it placed at a slight pitch running down and away from the window—about ⅛ of an inch down for a sill 4 inches wide is all that is needed so that water will roll off instead of pool up and stagnate. In addition to looking great, the sill will also act as a small and useful shelf. And while the pitch of the sill will be great enough to remove water, it won't be enough to tip over a bottle of shampoo or a bar of soap.

The grand total of this nifty bathroom accent piece might be $100, which should be enough to cover the cost of the stone, the fabrication, and any additional work in setting it below the window. If you're having tile setters work on your bathroom countertop or any other part of your house, they'll probably have access to their own stockpile of stone scraps and will be able to do it for even less.

Mechanics of Ventilation

Windows are the key to keeping a bathroom steam-free in warm weather, but this is of little use in the chill of winter. Chances are when the weather is 20 degrees below zero, as it is here in Chicago on many January mornings, you're not going to care about moisture problems if it means standing naked in an Arctic blast. In order to keep the bathroom free of moisture under these conditions, you need mechanical assistance in the form of a fan that vents directly outdoors.

The first step is to purchase a good-quality fan, which might cost $200 or even more. You can, of course, find discount fans for $25, but the motor on a contraption such as this has all the power of a motor you would find on a radio-controlled car at a toy store. These fans tend to move very little air, which is bad enough. In addition, they're noisy. It's a lose-lose situation. You won't even be able to hear yourself think when you're standing inside the bathroom, because of all the noise, and the little wisp of air moved by the fan will hardly make a dent in the tropical conditions within.

Instead, for the additional money, you will be buying a high-quality fan built with a large drum blower, which is similar to the kind found in forced–hot air heating systems. This moves a lot of air, *and* will never quit. True, it's more money—and in a bathroom renovation, every bill with Benjamin Franklin on it counts—but think of it as insurance to protect the rest of your investment in this room. You should also be prepared to spend another $300 or more for the connection, which involves electrical work as well as installing tubing to connect to the outside vent.

How do you choose a good fan? Unless you're an engineer and willing to study ratings and manuals, I think the best way to do this is to shop by brand, since good manufacturers tend to make good fans across all price ranges. Broan is one of the biggest manufacturers, as well as its sister company, NuTone. Panasonic, for its part, makes one of the quietest fans I've ever heard—or, I should say, ever *not* heard. In my own house I have

A Fan with a Mind of Its Own

According to the Home Ventilating Institute (who knew there was such a thing?) you're supposed to run your fan for twenty minutes following bathroom use—and thirty minutes, I would suggest, if you had chili the night before. While in theory this seems obvious, in practice this is often difficult to remember—if not for you, then for other less-home-improvement-savvy members of your household. Luckily there are several good solutions.

Some fans, notably those made by Broan, NuTone, and Panasonic, are equipped with humidity sensors that automatically switch the fan on and off to achieve the perfect moisture level. Another approach has been newly developed by GE, which is a thirty-minute timer switch for the wall that operates the fan. The switch retails for about $20, and the rectangular touch pad is divided up into four quadrants marked 5 minutes, 10 minutes, 15 minutes, and 30 minutes. With a touch of the button you can select the amount of time the fan should stay on, and then you can leave. The fan will shut off automatically when the time is up.

Whichever approach you take, you'll never have to nag anyone about turning on the fan again.

Broan fans in the bathrooms on the first and second floors, and in the basement bathroom I have a Panasonic. Although it moves a fair amount of air, you literally cannot hear it run.

To complicate matters, you also have to think about choosing the right size of fan for your bathroom. A fan is rated according to its CFM, which refers to the amount of air it can move measured in cubic feet per minute. According to the experts, a fan should have the capacity to completely change the air in the bathroom about ten times per hour in order to provide effective ventilation. Finding the volume of the room is easy. Just think back to sixth-grade math class and multiply the length and width of the room by the height. A 7-by-10-foot bathroom, with 8-foot ceilings, for example, contains 560 cubic feet. Multiply that by 10 times per hour and you will have 5,600, which is the amount of air measured in cubic feet that needs to be

The Sones of Silence

Fans are rated by their quietness, or lack of quietness, which is called a sone rating. Good-quality fans have better motors and make less noise—and have a lower sone rating. Cheap fans have noisy, vibrating motors—and hence, have a higher sone rating. For a 100 CFM fan, $50 might get you one with a sone rating of 4.5. Avoid this the way you would a package of rotten peppers on the discount produce shelf. By contrast, a $150 fan might have a sone rating of 2.5, which makes it a far better value.

moved each hour. Divide this by 60 minutes and you'll have the volume of air that needs to be moved each minute—the all-important CFM—which, in this case, is 93. The manufacturers will tell you that a fan rated at 100 CFM will be more than sufficient in this case.

I like to take bigger precautions, since in my opinion the manufacturers' calculations lead people to buy fans that are too small for the ventilation task at hand. I believe the smallest of bathrooms, such as the classic 5 by 7, need fans that move well over 100 CFM, not the 40 or 50 CFM the manufacturers' calculations would indicate. Their formulas were obviously designed by someone who has never lingered more than thirty seconds in the shower. Go ahead and do the calculations to come up with the CFM rating you need, then double it to be on the safe side. Although it will cost you marginally more, the installation costs will be identical. In the end, you'll end up with a fan you know is going to be more than adequate, and when it comes to ventilation, too much is a very good thing.

Installing a Fan

Okay, so now you have a fan—how do you install it? The first step is to choose a location in the ceiling. Since a fan pulls away odors as well as humidity, the best approach is to place it midway between the shower and bathtub area and the toilet. This allows the fan to do its job with maximum efficiency.

If you have a steam shower, which I'll discuss in greater detail in Chapter 5, you'll need a separate fan to handle all the humidity. The principle behind the steam shower, after all, is that the glass doors seal up, and so much moisture is pumped in that it literally becomes an indoor greenhouse; it's like a human hydroponics experiment in the master bath suite. Though you want all the steam trapped in there for the duration of your shower, you want to make sure it evacuates as soon as you're done. Otherwise, your bathroom walls are going to resemble a Chia Pet from all the things that start to sprout on them. A separate exhaust fan dedicated to just the steam shower is essential. In large bathrooms, the toilet is sometimes enclosed in a compartment, which is the classic water closet or WC. In this case, you would also want an additional fan located in that compartment because even though the room may not generate any steam, it will generate odors that won't air out on their own.

Besides positioning the fans, the other half of the problem is to fit the vent tubing that attaches to the fan. This has to be connected outside, so that moisture can be removed from the house completely. The vent will be covered with an exterior flap, similar to the one that you find on the outside cover of a clothes dryer.

A Secure Fan

Bathroom fans can be noisy, but much of this is because of vibrations caused by poor installation. To reduce noise, make sure you mount the fan securely to the framing of the bathroom, not just through the drywall. Be sure the housing is securely fastened on both sides with screws, which grab tightly even when vibrated, rather than nails, which don't.

Sometimes, homeowners who don't know better and contractors who want to cut corners try to vent the fan directly up and into the attic. The humidity literally blasts up there and condenses, and does just as much damage as it would have done if it had stayed in the bathroom in the first place—especially in areas with cold winters, where the condensation effect is even more pronounced. This constant dampness creates a potential mildew-and-mold breeding ground. Worse, the water that accumulates on the underside of the roof can do real structural damage over time.

One thing to worry about—again in cold climate—is condensation within the tube. In all cases the tube should be rigid metal, which looks something like a stovepipe. Flexible hose that you find on a dryer is simply not adequate for this sort of application, since it won't hold up. But metal tubing presents some challenges of its own. Many times, people will install fans in a ceiling, then immediately attach a pipe that rises straight up above the insulated space. This has some advantages, because the short run of tubing means that the fan will move air more efficiently. On the flip side, moisture can condense inside the pipe, and then it begins dripping back into the tubing and back through the fan and right onto the bathroom floor. As fast as you can pull moisture from the room, it seems, it rains right back down. Not only is this fairly revolting to anyone standing beneath it, you also run the risk of damaging the fan motor—since it was surely not designed to be saturated.

The solution to this lies in some clever placement of the piping. Where it attaches to the fan, the tubing should be connected to a 90-degree elbow pipe and should run straight for a good 2—or better yet, 3—feet along the backside of the plaster or drywall ceiling. This should be covered with insulation to protect the metal from extreme cold, which will buffer the cooling of the humid air in winter. That way, the moisture in it won't condense all at once. Then, instead of rising with an immediate 90-degree turn upward to vent outward, you gradually raise the pipe up to the roof using two 45-degree elbows. Although moisture will still condense on the inside of the pipe, it won't be to the same degree. And since it won't begin condensing until after it passes through the insulation, some 3 feet away from the fan, water won't be able to drip back down through the fan.

Warmth Beneath the Feet

Staying cool in a bathroom is usually not much of a problem, but staying warm certainly is. In order to be comfortable in a bathroom, you need to be warm, in part because you spend so much of your time in there without clothes on. This is a challenge because the principal material in a bathroom is tile, whether stone or ceramic—neither of which is a material known for its inherent warmth. In fact, ice cubes exude about as much chilliness as these surfaces do. To make these surfaces comfortable to the touch in colder months requires some thinking that goes beyond the basic heating system, whether you use a boiler with hot water heat or a furnace to produce forced hot air.

If it were possible to heat the bathroom separately from the rest of the house, this would make a lot of sense in terms of your overall comfort. That's because the bathroom is such a radically different space from any other part of your home. But though you can't change the laws of physics regarding the heating of materials that simply don't want to retain heat, you *can* work with your existing heating systems to create something much better. Let me walk you through some of the steps of how it can be done.

If you have forced hot air, the challenge is perhaps the greatest of all. Hot air rises, as we all know, and when it's piped into the bathroom, it wants to rise instantly to the ceiling rather than hang around toward the cold tile floor where you're standing. The goal with forced air heat, then, is to bring the heat in low so that the vent is either directly in the floor or fairly close to it. This will help warm some of the surfaces the hot air hits along the way, such as the floor—and even the bathtub or shower, if the vent is positioned well. Some of the nicest heat installations I've seen, in fact, include heat registers that are near the toilet. The heated air actually warms the porcelain of the toilet, which makes sitting down a much

A Radiant Joy

Large bathrooms seem to call out for beautiful floor finishes, from shiny marble to the sheen of limestone or tile. Yet step on any one of these surfaces with bare feet in the winter and the reaction is sure to be an icy chill. To remedy this, I recommend adding, especially in large bathrooms, radiant floor heat: heating coils that are placed under the tiles, which gently warm the surface of the floor itself, making it a joy to step on.

If you live in a house with a boiler, the best and cheapest solution is to install tubing called PEX, which can be laid in a serpentine fashion directly beneath the tiles, and carries a warm pulse of water beneath the surface. If you have forced-hot air heating, you're out of luck with PEX. You still have an option, however, in the form of an electric coil. Several companies market a thin electric warming mat that can be laid between the subfloor and the tiles. Run by a timer, the mat can be set to warm the floor just enough to keep toes toasty.

In my own bathroom, I added electric coils in the floor in a 6-by-8-foot mat right outside the shower. It's controlled by a timer, which I set to switch on at 4:30 A.M. so that when I step into the bathroom a half hour later, the floor is warm. The timer shuts the mat off at 9 A.M., after everyone has left for the day, then switches on again at 8 P.M. for another three hours. Although the cost was fairly expensive—about $500 for everything installed—the cost of running the mat is fairly cheap since it uses only about 250 watts, or the equivalent of four lightbulbs.

less shocking experience. Repositioning the registers in this way is easy to do during a whole-bathroom makeover. It can also be done, however, during a simpler renovation that may involve just a small amount of retiling or wall repair.

If your home has a boiler, you most likely have hot water heat, which also has some drawbacks in terms of heating a bathroom. Still, this can be reconfigured with an eye—or, I should say, a foot—toward maximum

Keeping Your Cool

Bathrooms tend to be cool in the summer, particularly if they are filled with stone or ceramic tiles. Still, central air-conditioning may be needed in some climates. Air-conditioning systems typically contain two parts: the airflow that forces cool air into a room; and the cold air return, which pulls air out to recirculate it. In bathrooms, however, there is typically no cold air return, which prevents moisture from being sucked into the air-conditioning system. The problem is that this also reduces the effectiveness of the air-conditioning. To compensate for this, make sure your bathroom airflow register is oversized so that you're getting the maximum possible volume of cold air—which will be something that will require the help of a heating and cooling contractor.

comfort. Many older houses and apartments with hot water heat contain bathrooms with old-fashioned cast-iron radiators. The problem with big radiators, however, is that they are slow to heat up, and take up a ton of space in the bathroom. This can be a problem especially in a small bathroom, where you're literally fighting for every square inch. Instead, it makes sense when remodeling to remove these big radiators and retrofit a hot water baseboard heater in the bathroom, which is much smaller and more streamlined. And it won't cost you anything in terms of comfort, either, because it will still offer the same amount of heating capacity, or even more. One caution: If you live in an apartment building, make sure you get management approval before proceeding.

Don't settle for just any baseboard heat, however. With hot water heat, you typically have two choices when it comes to baseboard heaters. One type is called a fin-tube element, which is essentially a ¾-inch hot water copper pipe decorated with small metal fins, then wrapped in a steel enclosure. The fins cause the hot water pipe to "lose" heat into the room. For anyone who has studied prehistoric creatures with their children, as I have, this is the same principle that governs the way the plates on the

Stegosaurus are believed to have radiated heat to keep the animal cool and absorbed heat to keep it warm. When the heating element is turned on, the room heats up quickly, but it cools down just as quickly when the heat clicks off, because nothing stores the heat at all. The dinosaur angle is an apt one when it comes to metal fin tubes, because you can do much better than this fossil in the bathroom—and the answer lies in cast iron.

Clunky as they are, one of the advantages of the old cast-iron radiators is that even though they do take a little bit of time to heat up, once they are warmed up and the boiler shut down, they stay warm for a long time afterward. If you're frying bacon in a cast-iron pan, you know the pan stays hot long after you've turned the flame off. In radiators, cast iron offers this same advantage. You don't have to add old-fashioned heaters in your bathroom, however. Instead, you can add smaller baseboard versions of these, which contain cast-iron elements that literally become a reservoir of heat. These baseboard heaters can be painted to blend into the room, and the only way you would know they're there is because of the even temperature within the room.

Although cast-iron baseboard heat makes a great solution for keeping a bathroom comfortable, it does come at a small cost. Metal fin tubes would probably cost you between $6 to $10 a running foot, but cast-iron baseboards will probably cost you $25 to $35 per foot. If you were outfitting the entire house in cast-iron baseboard heaters you

Proof in Numbers

A radiator's performance is rated in terms of British thermal units, or BTUs, per hour, which is a measure of the amount of heat it gives off. The higher the BTUs, the more comfortable you'll be in a bathroom. Filled with 190-degree water, a 4-foot section of a metal fin tube radiator releases about 1,300 BTUs per hour. By contrast, the same water pumping through a 4-foot section of a cast-iron baseboard radiator releases twice the amount of heat, or about 2,600 BTUs per hour. This makes cast iron a far better choice.

might balk at the price difference, but keep in mind the small scale of most bathrooms. At the most, the cost difference for a 4-foot section of a baseboard radiator would be about $100. It's a great little extra—and one that you'll remember every time you step into the bathroom on a cold morning.

It's small details such as these that make a huge difference in the way a bathroom works, without breaking the budget. Follow me now as we untangle another difficult area you're likely to confront—the plumbing system.

chapter THREE

Pipe Dreams

What's the secret to a perfect bathroom? Perfect plumbing—with no leaks and plenty of hot water.

A simple bathroom makeover can sometimes turn into an accidental full-scale remodeling, as my partner Mike and I found out the hard way some years ago.

When we first entered the contracting business, the two of us worked for a few different real estate agencies. Our job was to give houses on the market a quick makeover to help them sell faster. This usually involved minor things such as planing the occasional sticking door, or brushing on a badly needed coat of paint. One day we were sent to a house with what purported to be a simple problem: a clogged bathtub. The house had been vacant for some time, and was in awful condition all around. Whoever bought the house would inevitably be redoing the bathroom, the real estate agent thought, so there was no need trying to fix it all. Our job was just the tub.

Fumbling through our arsenal of plumbing tools—which amounted to a plumber's snake and a few wrenches—we tried to rout out the drain to clear it. No dice, and the water continued to sit there. Heading down into the basement, we found what is called a drum catch on the main drainpipe coming from the tub. This is sort of like a mini–grease trap you would find by the kitchen sink, only for the tub. Normally the process of cleaning out one of these things goes like this: You hold your breath, pull it open, clear it of any debris, close it back up, breathe a sigh of relief, and you're in business once again. Working with the wrench, I tried to pry the drum catch open, with no luck. I puffed up my chest and tried again and, finally, with one giant grunt, I went at it with all my might. This time, I succeeded in opening it up, all right—not the drum catch, that is, but the entire aged pipe. It literally busted open, and half a century's worth of gook and gray debris came spraying and slopping down on top of us. "Nice work," said Mike, ever the master of understatement.

As if this weren't bad enough, it turns out that we had literally opened Pandora's plumbing box. The problem was that the water pipes were

A Bathroom Down Under

In our never-ending quest for more living space, many of us turn our eyes down to the basement. It offers huge possibilities—as long as you manage any wetness problems first—and makes a great place for a spare bathroom. In most ways, a basement bathroom is the same as any other bathroom, except for one thing: You need an ejector pump, and fast.

Upstairs in a house, wastewater from sinks, toilets, and showers is fed by gravity to the main sewer line. What happens, however, if a laundry room or bathroom is in the basement, where the drain lies below the main sewer line? Wastewater can't jump, so it needs something to lift it up and out of the house. This requires what is called an ejector pump, which is contained inside an ejector pit that is embedded into the basement floor. This pit is identical to the pit for

a sump pump, except that the cover is sealed to prevent sewer gases from escaping. It contains a flotation ball similar to what you would find in the tank of a toilet that triggers the pump to start as the pit fills. When it switches on, out goes the waste.

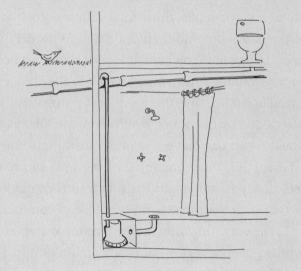

made of galvanized iron pipe—common in older homes—which deteriorates over time. As it turned out, all the old joints connecting the various sections of piping were thin and crumbly. We touched one fitting to try to fix the leak we had created, and that one started to leak, too. Then we went back 3 feet to the next fitting to try that, only to have that one spring a leak, as well. On and on it went, until we felt like Mo and Curly from *The Three Stooges*. Within an hour it became clear that there was no way to fix what we had started, since every single pipe we touched—from the water supply pipes to the drainpipes—began to disintegrate. We had to replace everything, and over the course of a few days the house had brand-new plumbing in the basement. Eventually the real estate agent stopped by to see how things were coming with the tub, and wanted to know if we would be interested in doing a straightforward renovation of the bathroom. Since half the job was finished because we had already installed new plumbing, we eagerly agreed. Saved!

Bathroom renovations seem like one of those things that should be contained in a single area. Yet, as we discovered, much of the work goes on downstairs in the basement. That's where the main sections of the plumbing system lie, those vital connections that bring hot and cold water to the bathroom and then drain away waste. Plumbing is the essence of a great bathroom. You need it for hot water and cold water, and in plentiful supply. Who wants to stand naked in the shower only to have a few drips sprinkle out because there's no water pressure? Conversely, who wants to be scalded by hot water when someone flushes the toilet elsewhere in the house? You can have the most beautiful fixtures and tiling found anywhere, but if the plumbing isn't modern and ready to go, you're going to feel as if you're back in the nineteenth century—with one exception: An outhouse at least makes no pretense of comfort.

Let's work through the bathroom water and drain lines, beginning with an overview of what exactly plumbing is. This will help guide you in the choices you need to make, and help you understand why all those checks you'll be writing to the plumber are essential.

What Are All These Pipes?

Because most of the pipes are hidden in the walls, homeowners tend to have a slightly warped view of the plumbing system. Water comes out of the faucet, and disappears down the drain. Hot water comes from

On the Move

There are certain things that are fixed in this world: Earth revolves around the Sun; the Chicago Cubs will never win the pennant (hey, there's always next year!); and you can never afford to move the plumbing once it's in place. But one of these is wrong—and, sorry, sports fans, it's not the one concerning my beloved Cubs.

Although you won't be able to move the plumbing in a simple renovation, there are no rules when it comes to a more involved gut rehab. Once everything is stripped down to the bare studs, any plumbers worthy of their tool buckets will be able to reconfigure things exactly as you want. This sometimes comes as news to homeowners, since people tend to be constrained by the thought that everything has to go back where it came from. I recently had a conversation with a woman in Arizona, for instance, who had a house built on a concrete slab. She wanted to create a handicap-accessible shower without a barrier, but wasn't sure how to do it in the tiny space she had. The obvious answer was to move the drain by breaking up the floor and repositioning it. When I told her this, it was as if I were telling her to change one of the Ten Commandments, until a lightbulb clicked on. "You mean, you can move things like a drain?" she asked.

Yes, you can. And though you will pay more for it—probably between $500 to $800, in her case—you have to put it in a broader perspective. The lifespan of a well-done bathroom can be easily fifteen to twenty years, and there's no reason it can't last twenty-five. Spending a few thousand dollars up front to rearrange the plumbing in order to create the space you need is well worth the effort.

the handle on the left; cold water comes from the right. End of the story.

Not quite. Although this little bit of knowledge is more than satisfactory to get through day-to-day life, it hardly suffices when a renovation of the bathroom turns into a plumbing job, as well. Suddenly, you're confronted with a contractor talking about supply lines and vent pipes, the need for a new main drain, and tossing out prices that seem like they're the punch lines to jokes. New supply lines? $4,000. New main sewer line? $10,000. A total plumbing overhaul? Priceless. This is what home equity lines of credit were born for, as well as, perhaps, the lottery. Know one thing before you start: It costs far more to tinker with the plumbing in an existing bathroom than it does to install it in a new house, because the plumber has to maneuver around so many obstacles. To help you know what you're getting and what you need—and to help you get it at a realistic price—let's take a quick tour of the plumbing system. This is actually two entirely separate systems that work in tandem. One is the water supply system, which is self-explanatory, and the other is the drain-waste-vent system, or DWV, which is not.

Let's start with the supply side, where water enters the house. Your water supply comes from either a well or the public water supply system. Now, the key to water is that it has to flow under pressure—pressure great enough to raise it to gravity-defying heights, such as the second-

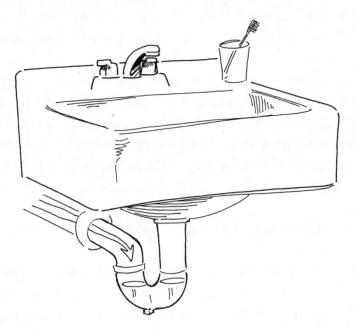

A Concise Guide to Plumbing

Plumbing consists of two completely separate systems. The first is the water supply, which brings water into the house, heats it, then pipes it into a faucet, where it awaits someone to turn it on. The second part is the drain-waste-vent system, or DWV, which removes *wastewater* from the house and prevents sewer gases from belching back into it. Like yin and yang, these two systems form two entirely separate parts of a whole—and one can't function without the other.

floor master bathroom. With a well, this is supplied by a pump. In a public water supply system, however, water is often piped up to water holding tanks, which are those giant contraptions that dot the landscape. The normal pressure for water running through the pipe is between 30 and 60 pounds per square inch (psi). Once it reaches the inside of your home, some of the water is diverted to a water heater and then continues onward. Turn on the faucet, and there it is. The water supply system has done its job.

Once you use the water, of course, it has to have someplace to go—and this is where the drain-waste-vent system comes into play. This is a completely separate system from the supply, and is connected to the sink, the drain in the tub and shower, the base of the toilet bowl, and anywhere else that water flows. Whereas the supply system flows under pressure, the drain-waste-vent system flows by gravity alone. Just as the mighty Mississippi gathers up strength from countless tributaries, so the main drainpipe that runs vertically in the house is fed by small-diameter pipes that connect to these various fixtures. The main drain empties straight down to the basement, then out to either the public sewer system or into the septic tank and septic field.

Simple enough, right? There is one complicating factor. In the drain-waste-vent system, sewer gases can bubble back up into the house, which would not be pleasant, to say the least. In fact, this is the reason why people spent so many centuries with outhouses instead of indoor plumbing. They could figure out how to pump water into the house, and also how to drain wastewater out, but they just couldn't figure out how to escape the ghastly odors. Today, we've got a solution. This is in the form of the curved pipes, underneath the sinks and faucets, called the P-trap. This traps water, which acts as a cork that literally blocks gases and prevents them from burping back into the house. You should thank daily the anonymous inventor of this ingenious configuration. A necessary companion to the P-trap is a vent system, which consists of those little stacks that protrude from the roof of your house. You may have thought these connect to the exhaust vents in the bathroom or kitchen, but they do not. Instead, these vents bring air into the system to allow wastewater to drain faster, and also allow any gases that accumulate to vent in a location unlikely to cause anyone distress—namely, up in the sky.

Under Pressure

A retired client of mine named Marvin always managed to see the beauty in things that other homeowners wanted to cover up, right down to the plumbing.

A case in point was his reaction to a visit from the plumber during a

A Two-Second Guide to Plumbing

How do you find out in two seconds if your home needs a plumbing overhaul? That's simple: Find out how old the house is. If you're living in a brand-new house, or one built within the past forty years, there's good news: You probably don't have much to worry about, and can simply make changes in the bathroom as you need to, without a total overhaul. Unlike electrical systems, plumbing systems haven't really changed in the last fifty years. For anyone with an older house, however, you're very likely going to have some issues to sort out.

How Much Is *That* Going to Cost?

There are two ways to balance the finances during a renovation. One is to act like an accountant and keep careful records of estimates and actual costs. The other is to close your eyes and hope for the best. Like many people, I tend to want to know what something will cost before I commit to it, and this list can help you out with a general idea. If you do the work yourself, you can accumulate big savings over the cost of having a professional do the job for you. Just make sure you get some advance training and set aside enough time to do the job right. Otherwise, you're going to be paying twice—once to mess the job up yourself, and again to have someone come in and correct things.

Installing a new sink and faucet.
Do-It-Yourself: $400
Professional: $1,000

Installing a shower surround.
Do-It-Yourself: $200
Professional: $1,500

Installing a toilet.
Do-It-Yourself: $150
Professional: $600

Changing the valve and faucet on a shower or tub.
Do-It-Yourself: $100
Professional: $400

Installing a bathtub.
Do-It-Yourself: Don't even attempt this!
Professional: $1,000 to $1,500

Septic Systems 101

If you have a septic system rather than a public sewer connection, it's a good time to ask yourself this question while you're renovating your bathroom: "When did we last have the septic tank pumped out?" If you don't know the answer to this, the chances are good that it's time to do something about it.

Septic tanks are designed to accumulate what are politely called "solids," while liquid waste then drains off and dissipates harmlessly through the septic field nearby. Gross, I know, but this is something that you can't close your eyes to. If the tank fills up with solids, they start sloughing off into the piping of the septic field, and can plug it up and damage it. This is a completely avoidable situation, and one that would cost many thousands of dollars to repair. To prevent this, the tank needs to be pumped out every three to five years, depending on its size and the volume of use. The process will cost as little as $65—which, considering the task at hand, has to rank as one of the world's great bargains. To find someone, look in the telephone directory under "septic" and don't worry about checking references. This is one job that anyone who attempts it will assuredly do well.

No one is going to remind you that this maintenance project needs to be done, the way you get a notice telling you your taxes are due, or the furnace or boiler needs cleaning. But it *is* something that's essential to the well-run home.

massive bathroom renovation. This involved all new plumbing to the room, and an upgrade of every system. That was the easy part. In addition, Marvin wanted a steam shower, which involved a few days' work by Donny the plumber. Instead of using plastic supply lines, which are commonly allowed in many areas today, Donny preferred to work with copper tubing. He attached it to the half-dozen or so nozzles that connected to the steam shower. Now, I've always considered Donny some-

Plumbing without Ticks

Maybe you've heard this sound. You take a shower, and you hear a ticking noise. What is it? It's not an alarm clock. Instead, it's a sign that the copper piping has been fastened to the framing with metal strapping. As the hot water pipe heats up, it expands and rubs against the stripping—with a steady tick, tick, tick sound. When it cools, you hear the same thing. An easy way to avoid this during a renovation is to wrap the pipe where it meets the metal stripping with a layer of spongy neoprene, which is a thin foam material that comes in little sheets. The neoprene helps take the noise out of the expansion and contraction.

thing of an artist; he is to plumbing what, say, Kenneth Cole is to shoes. Sure, his piping gets the job done—but it also looks so much better than anyone else's. When he was finished, the plumbing wall glimmered with beautifully symmetrical copper coils, which almost looked like sculpture.

Marvin noticed this immediately, even before he noticed the steam shower itself. "This is beautiful, just beautiful!" he exclaimed, and at first didn't want me to cover anything up with drywall so we could get on with the project. "No, we have to have this on display," he said, and he meant it. He wondered if we could cover it with Plexiglas for everyone to see, as a sort of monument to fine plumbing. Everyone, including Donny, talked him out of this. As a compromise, we took some photos. I'm not sure if he ever enlarged one and framed it, but he did speak of doing that. Not all of us may be able to appreciate the beauty of a plumbing system

Plumb Deals

Given the costs of renovation, we all try to cut expenses. There are good ways and bad ways to do this. The bad ways will lead to regret, because you will ultimately compromise both the quality and the usefulness of your bathroom—by scrimping on essentials, such as good plumbing and upgraded heating and ventilation systems. Good ways to cut costs, however, include the following:

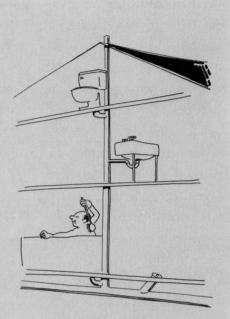

- If you have a choice, locate bathrooms back to back, or stacked one above the other. This is a classic building technique that minimizes the costs by consolidating and minimizing the amount of plumbing required.

- If you're building a new house or an addition and can't afford to put a bathroom in the basement right away, have the plumbing "roughed in," anyway, so that the water lines and waste lines are set in place. This will greatly reduce the cost of adding a bathroom in the future, and will be a good selling point to your house even if you never actually add the bathroom yourself.

- Instead of tile surrounds for the tub and shower, choose acrylic liners that cut the costs practically in half. These look good, and have an added bonus in that they create what is practically a maintenance-free bathroom.

- If you're installing more than one bathroom, choose the same fixtures for each one. Not only will you be able to get a discount for buying in bulk, but your contractor will be able to install them more quickly, which will save you money.

with this same degree of fanaticism, but we all can certainly appreciate its mechanical perfection.

How a system works forms the core of a well-done bathroom. The key to a plumbing system lies in maintaining water pressure so that water rushes out with vigor, rather than trickling on top of you as you stand in the shower. Fueling all this is the plumbing system's main supply pipe, or riser, which runs to the bathroom. This pipe, which usually measures ¾ to 1 inch in diameter, brings the water directly to the bathroom. It's like the trunk of some watery tree, and from here it branches off. Smaller supply pipes with diameters as small as ½ an inch lead to the toilet, the vanity, the shower, and the tub. Each of these carries water to a different fixture and, as it does, the pressure of the water within the pipe drops.

For these pipes, there's a great deal of debate about what the proper choice of materials is—from CPVC plastic pipes to copper. Much of these debates centers on the issue of cost, not performance. For me, there is only one choice, and that's copper piping. I think copper pipes are the best choice because they are easy to work with and are one of the longest-lasting materials. In addition, they tend to stay clearer and open longer than any other pipes, such as the old-fashioned galvanized iron or even plastic pipes. Additionally, plastic pipes can leave a plastic taste in your drinking water, and who wants that? By contrast, copper pipes survive for decades without the slightest wear, and without leaving any taste in the water itself. Just take a look at an old penny—it holds up, no matter what. Many municipalities and cities require copper piping, so you really have no choice. But others allow plastic piping, and this is where you have to make sure that a contractor will upgrade to copper. In all cases, I believe, you should go with copper piping for the supply system because it's just the best way to add value to your home. Plastic water pipes, to me, just don't exude quality.

The volume of water is the most important thing in a supply system. Water volume determines the amount of water pressure you have in your shower and throughout your entire home. Pressure is a strange thing, because you can't really add to it. Water comes into your home at a certain pressure, or is pumped from the well at a certain pressure, and that's that. Older homes typically have a ¾-inch main feed water into the home, and chances are they don't have the greatest water pressure. If you connect this ¾-inch line to a 1-inch pipe common in newer houses to supply the rest of the house, you're not going to get any more pressure. In fact, you're going to decrease the pressure drastically because suddenly the water has a larger diameter pipe to flow through. It's a little like the difference between a river rushing through a narrow gorge, then gliding serenely through a pool.

To conserve water pressure in these systems, you want to make sure the water flows up to the bathroom in as straight a route as possible. Any elbows and turns will reduce the pressure, as well as the flow. Once this pipe reaches the bathroom, the water pressure is reduced because of the gravity acting against it. To keep the flow constant, the pipes leading into the valves and faucets are restricted farther from ¾ of an inch to ½ an inch, depending on the system. Don't expect water to jet out, however. No matter what, the federal Environmental Protection Agency (EPA) mandates that faucets can produce a maximum of only 2.2 gallons per minute. If sorting out these pipes sounds confusing, it is; this is a job for a plumber, and perhaps even an engineer. In addition, plumbing systems have something called compression chambers hidden in the wall near each faucet. They're filled with air, not water, and they provide a cushion to soften the abrupt halt to the flow of water when the faucet is turned off. Think of them as bumpers for the water supply. A compression chamber in the water pipe absorbs the impact, and eliminates any vibration and noise.

Over time, however, the air in these compression chambers may become displaced by water. This becomes obvious if you turn off a faucet and hear a bone-rattling knocking sound, which ranks as one of the most irritating problems in home plumbing systems. The cure is an easy one, however. The trick is to turn off the main water supply valve right where water enters the house, and then to turn on every faucet to drain the system entirely. Once the faucets stop dripping, turn them off and turn the main valve back on to slowly refill the supply system. Once the system sputters and spits its way back to normal, the air in the compression chambers will have been restored—and you should have knock-free plumbing once again.

The Sounds of Silence

I have a confession, which by now shouldn't seem too shocking, and that is this: Not everything runs perfectly in my home. Every time I'm in the kitchen and one of my children flushes the toilet upstairs, I hear the water rushing down the main drainpipe. It's like fingernails on the chalkboard—and would have been easy to prevent had I only been there when the plumber was installing it. Though I have to live with this mistake, I'm going to explain the simple solution to make sure you don't have the same problem.

Everyone wants plumbing that works well, but no one especially wants to hear about it. A flushing of the pipes, especially through a living room or near a guest room, can be cause for embarrassment. Whereas the toilet and sink do make noise while in operation, the really offending sounds are produced when wastewater flows through the main drainpipe down and out of the house. The waste spills through the pipe with a gigantic splash, similar to the sound of water plunging off the top of Niagara Falls, although far less scenic. The solution lies in the choice of material used for the drainpipe.

Ordinarily, this pipe is made from PVC plastic—those thick white pipes familiar to anyone who

A Place for Plastics

Although cast iron makes a far better material than plastic for the main drainpipe, plastic is a fine and cost-effective choice for the smaller 2-inch drainpipes that connect the sink to the main drain as well as the 3-inch pipe that comes from the toilet. It is only the larger pipe that should be made of cast iron.

has strolled through the aisles of a home improvement store. This is distinct from the similar-sounding but chemically different CPVC piping, which is used for water supply. The beauty of PVC pipe is that it's sturdy, it will never leak, and it will do the job. Plus, it's cheap and easy to work with, which is why people love it. A 10-foot section of drainpipe might cost $20, making this the material of choice for any builder who is mass-producing houses. The problem is, these pipes have all the acoustical integrity of a piece of paper. In fact, they almost seem to augment the sounds coming from within, as if it were some sort of septic echo chamber. This is what I hear in my kitchen in the morning, and this is what is eminently preventable.

A far better material for the main drainpipe is cast iron. This is the material first used when bathrooms moved indoors, and it makes the best choice today. Cast iron, which is distinct from the old, galvanized iron used as supply pipes, has an enormous density to it compared to the PVC piping. As a result, it contains the sounds within it to a huge degree. If you put your ear to the wall, you can hear a faint rush when this pipe is in use, but it is far from the conversation-stopping roar of the plastic pipes. True, cast-iron piping costs you somewhat more. A 10-foot section would cost about $40, compared to $20 for the plastic version. Installation is also slightly more expensive, since it requires more skill to attach the fittings. The total extra charge might amount to $100, but this is worth every penny.

If you don't use cast iron for this drainpipe, you can try to wrap the plastic pipe with ordinary Fiberglas insulation in an attempt to deaden the sound—but it doesn't offer much protection. Believe me, I've tried it.

Are You in Hot Water?

Here's a scenario that I've heard about one too many times. A home-owner decides to add a giant whirlpool tub to his or her bathroom, and imagines coming home from work and soaking away all the stresses and strains of the day. The hot water comes churning out of the faucet at first, but before the tub is even 4 inches full, it's colder than a glass of iced tea in August.

Although you can get away with a limited amount of hot water in the kitchen—after all, just how many gallons does it take to fill a sink?—the same is not true in the bathroom. Fill up the tub, or take a long shower, or try to have an entire family get ready for the day at the same time, and the hot water could run out. Guaranteeing a steady supply of hot water when you want it is a major factor in a bathroom's success, and here's how I think you should go about it.

Everyone is familiar with the conventional water heater in their basement, that round cylinder that looks something like a gigantic roll of paper towels. Though getting a water heater large enough to supply hot water to your tub is an essential requirement, determining the right size requires some mind-bending calculations, as well as an understanding of how water heaters work. First, let's start with the mechanics. In the tanks, the heating element lies at the base, whether the source of heat is electricity or a boiler fueled by gas or oil. Take yourself back to sixth-grade science class, and review the theory that hot air, as well as hot water,

What's in a Name?

The standard name for the device that heats water in a home is the hot water heater. But this is a misnomer, since, if the water is hot, why would you need a device to heat it? Ideally, these devices should be called cold water heaters, but I would settle for an even simpler form: water heaters.

rises and gathers toward the top of the water heater. If you don't use any hot water for an hour or so, the entire tank then contains uniformly hot water. But the moment you turn on the hot water faucet somewhere in the house, cold water is drawn into the bottom of the tank. Although the burner or heating element also kicks on at the same time, it does not heat this water instantaneously. This means that the more hot water you draw from the tank, the more cold water is pulled into it. Although this does not affect the temperature of the water at first, the cold water eventually dilutes the hot water and reduces the temperature of water flowing from the tap. At first, the water might spill out at a steamy 120 degrees, but then drop to 90 degrees as the dilution effect kicks in.

This principle is important to consider when choosing the appropriate size of water heater for your needs—and it is something that people almost always underestimate. If you have a 75-gallon whirlpool tub, which is perhaps the average two-person tub, you might think that you'd need to fill it with 70 percent hot water and 30 percent cold water, which would require about 50 gallons of hot water. A 50-gallon tank should be sufficient, right? Wrong. The problem is that with a 50-gallon water heater, you're only going to get about 25 gallons of truly hot water at 120 degrees. By the time you get to that 26th gallon, you'll be lucky to get water at 100 degrees, and the temperature will continue to slide from there. So in order to fill a tub this size, you would need to have a 75-gallon water tank, unless you like the idea of luxuriating in tepid water.

Until now, the solution to this ever-increasing need for hot water was to add larger and larger water heaters. This is sort of the same thinking that led to the creation of the SUV, however, and with the same costly side effects. To put it briefly, water heaters cost a great deal of money to operate. It's one thing to have the burner kick on when you're actually using hot water. These tanks, however, are designed to create and store hot water without giving any thought to whether anyone will actually be using it. That means if you have a new 75-gallon tank in your basement

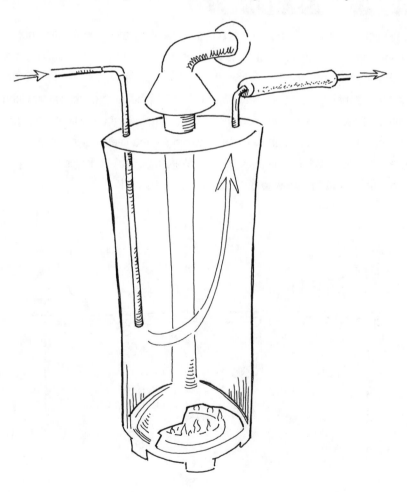

to handle that once-a-week whirlpool bath, you're paying to keep 75 gallons of hot water on hand every second of every day, whether you're asleep or at work. The water heater doesn't know you only need this amount of water one evening a week, and could probably get by with only about 10 gallons or even 5 gallons the rest of the week. It has one job: to keep that tank hot, and it does it with budget-breaking efficiency. The average water heater burns up about $300 worth of energy a year, which makes it more costly to operate than most refrigerators.

A Safer Way to Shower

Have you ever stood in the shower only to have the water turn scalding hot if someone turns on a faucet or flushes the toilet? The remedy for this annoying and potentially dangerous reality lies in anti-scald valves, which are also known as pressure-balancing valves. Required since 1988 by building codes for new construction, these valves employ sensing mechanisms designed to limit temperature fluctuations and prevent accidental scalding—and keep water temperature constant, usually within 3 degrees. They make a great safety device for every home—not just in the shower, but in the bathtub, as well.

Until recently, there hasn't been a solution to this water-heating problem— but I've found something that works very well. It's called the tankless water heater. This device operates just like a conventional water heater in terms of heating water, except for one important distinction: It does not store hot water at all. When you turn on the hot water tap, the burner kicks on and hot water is produced only as you use it. If you're washing your hands, the water heater quickly produces the pint of hot water you'd use. If you're filling the big soaking tub, it will keep pouring out hot water until the job is done. And then when you're done, it shuts off until you need more hot water again.

Tanks a Lot

If you're adding a large tub to a bathroom, one way to ensure it will have adequate hot water is to install a tankless water heater to service it. Although the rest of the plumbing in the house can draw from a conventional water heater tank, the large tub can draw from a tankless water heater. This guarantees you enough hot water—and prevents you from having to upgrade to a larger, energy-gobbling tank.

In terms of logic and energy-efficiency, nothing comes close to these tankless water heaters. They come in several sizes, as well, from those that produce about 3 gallons of hot water per minute—which is more than adequate to feed a low-flow showerhead—to those that can produce about 6 gallons of hot water per minute. This is the size you would need to fill a big tub. Although popular in Europe, where they originated, these tankless water heaters have been slow to catch on here, which has been puzzling to me. Some of the problem, obviously, has to do with their cost. While a standard water heater might cost $100 or $200 for one with a 40-gallon capacity, a tankless heater might run between $500 for the small ones that produce about 3 gallons of hot water per minute, and $1,000 for the large ones that produce 6 gallons per minute. But this is a misleading number, because the cost of running the tankless heaters is far less, and probably only about $125 a year on average for one with a 3-gallon-per-minute capacity. Since a 40-gallon standard water heater might cost about $300 a year to operate, this represents an annual savings in operating costs of about $175. At this rate, the tankless units would pay for themselves in energy savings in about three years.

With the plumbing system tidied away, let's get out the magnifying glass to take a close-up look at the most common surface material in a bathroom—tile.

chapter FOUR

Tile with Style

These squares of ceramic or stone make the best material for bathroom floors and walls—if they're properly installed.

When it comes to tiles, subtlety makes the best policy, with respect to color. This is a lesson some clients of mine were slow to learn.

Working with a crew a few years ago, I had the chance to work on a lavish house, easily costing $2 million. Although the house was extremely livable and beautiful, the master bathroom presented a giant problem—namely, the color of the tile. The couple wanted to do the entire bathroom in marble, from floors to walls, which was rather classy in itself. The color they chose for the tile, however, was not. It turned out to be pink. Not pink like cotton candy, perhaps, but nonetheless a hue too close to Pepto-Bismol for my comfort. I suggested my doubts about the color. "One single tile might look good, but I'm telling you, when you set this into an entire bathroom, you're asking for trouble," I cautioned them, but to no effect.

We tiled the place, anyway, box after box, paving the place into a vision of pink. The result was some Ivana Trump dream gone wild. The tile setter could barely spread on the mortar without laughing, but the couple said they loved it. That could have been the end of the story, I suppose, but within a couple of years the husband accepted a job transfer, and their house went on the market. It sold quickly, but the new owners asked for a price reduction to cover the cost of a new bathroom. Why? They couldn't stand the color, either, and had it gutted and replaced before they even moved in.

Tile is a remarkable surface for a bathroom, and tailor-made for the job it performs. More durable than vinyl or wood, it resists water and lasts practically forever because it simply will not rot. Just think about it: Archaeological expeditions have dug through ruins from ancient Babylonia, and what have they come up with? Chunks of tile that look as fresh as the day they were fired some four thousand years ago. Yet tile is only as strong as the wall or the floor behind it, and depends on the ever-critical grout line to keep it intact. In addition, tile becomes the focal point of the bathroom simply because there's so much of it. Yard upon yard of tile can blanket even the smallest of bathrooms, especially if a shower stall or bathtub surround is tiled, as well as the floors and portions of the wall. Before you know it, that one little square you looked at in the store has multiplied and multiplied again, presenting a concentrated color and texture that can be a shock if it's not carefully chosen. Because it forms such an integral and permanent surface in the bathroom, the color can't be changed without a major renovation.

Let's work through some of the options, from choosing tiles to having them installed correctly, so you can make educated choices that neither you nor anyone else will regret—for the entire life of your bathroom.

Being Choosy

Take a walk down the local home center tile aisle, and you'll be all but assaulted by the tile possibilities, from basic ceramic ones that recall high school gym showers, to hand-tumbled marble ones from Italy that resemble something from the halls of the Sistine Chapel. There are almost too many choices, and the possibility of making a mistake is enormous—as my clients

Tiles with a Difference

Want to build a distinctive bathroom? One way to accomplish this is to choose some unique tiles, and here are two of my favorites.

Among the most popular—and beautiful—of all bathroom tiles are those made of limestone. There are literally hundreds of colors and patterns of limestone on the market now, and most of them have a honed finish that gives them a warm look that's pleasing to touch. Polished limestone isn't used much, mostly because its surface looks too artificial, sort of like plastic. By contrast, travertine limestone has a pockmarked finish resulting from water that percolated through the stone as it formed in the earth. Be warned of one thing, though: Limestone is permeable to water, and thus can stain easily. The remedy lies in sealing it annually with a water repellent for extra protection.

Another type of tile that has been gaining popularity in recent years is made of recycled glass. Who knew that a chardonnay bottle, for instance, creates a celery-colored tile, whereas a clear juice bottle creates an opaque tile useful for countertops? In addition to being environmentally friendly, these tiles create a shimmery luminescence when used in showers and saunas, or on floors. The tile molds themselves are created from clay, then cast in iron and filled with molten glass. Although they sound as if they would be brittle, glass tiles are as sturdy as granite when installed—and are cut and set just like ceramic.

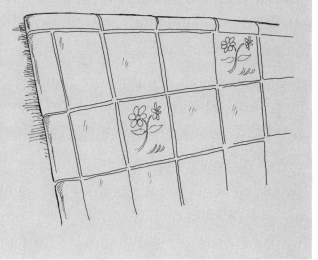

who went down the pink-tiled road discovered firsthand. I can't tell you what color schemes or choices will work for you, but I can give you some guidelines that should help prevent any colossal, and expensive, mistakes.

The most common and versatile tile material, of course, is ceramic. In fact, just say the word "bathroom" and these enameled squares are what most people envision. Although we tend to stick to basic shapes and colors, tiles come in a bewildering array of materials and styles. Broadly speaking, ceramic tiles, made from fired clay, are grouped according to their water permeability—from nonvitreous, which readily absorbs water, to semivitreous, vitreous, and impervious. The more impermeable clay tiles are fired at higher temperatures—upward of 2,000 degrees—which fuses the elements in them and makes them suitable for use in wet locations. Most have a waterproof glaze that adds to their durability. Ceramic tiles span the price range from those that are reduced on sale and cost less than a dollar per square foot, to handmade tiles that might cost hundreds.

Increasingly popular are natural stone tiles, which tend to cost much

The Vocabulary of Tiles

Want to sound like you know what you're talking about when you go to the tile showroom? Then take a moment to learn a few words that will have you speaking like an expert. Bathroom tiles themselves come in three distinct types. Field tiles are those that are set in the main portion of an installation, which make up the bulk of the tiles used on the floor or on the wall. Trim tiles have a distinctly shaped edge to them, and are used to build a border around the field tiles. They generally cost more per tile than field tiles, and come with names like "bull-nose" or "half-round" tiles. Finally, decorative or accent tiles are used sparingly. These can be hand-painted tiles, tiles of unusual materials, or can feature raised-relief shapes that bring to life a plain span of field tiles. Now that you sound like a bathroom decorator, who knows—maybe you can even ask for a designer's discount.

Want to wake up a bathroom? Do it with color, but in a way that isn't permanent. Go ahead: paint the walls purple, add orange wallpaper, and put in plaid towels and shower curtains. These are the things that are easy to change whenever you— or the next buyer of your house—want to. Just keep the colors of the permanent things, especially the tiles, reined in.

more than ceramic tiles but add a distinctive look to a bathroom. The first thing to consider with stone tiles is the finish, rather than the color. Some are glossy, which look beautifully reflective but also become extremely slippery when wet. These might work well in a half bath or powder room, but can tend to make a poor choice for the floor of a family bath. Better for this are stones with a more natural finish, called honed. These unfinished stones are naturally porous, and provide greater traction for anyone walking on them in bare feet. In showers and around bathtubs, however, the rough surface of these stones provides too many places for mold and mildew to take hold. Polished stones would be my choice in these areas, since they are easier to keep clean.

Color is obviously a major factor when choosing tiles. For this, follow my three rules to guarantee that you'll get it right: restrain yourself, restrain yourself, and restrain yourself. We've all had the experience of going to the paint store and choosing an entire bucket of paint based on how it looks on one little square. Then, after you've spent the weekend painting the room eggplant, or pomegranate, or tangerine, you've

A Turn of the Screw

Although cement board is essential to help a tile wall or floor hold up, there is a particular type of screw that is essential to hold up the cement board. Manufactured by ITW Buildex, it is a product called Rock-On—and should be the fastener of choice in any bathroom renovation.

Until recently, carpenters would simply nail the sheets of cement board in place, or use ordinary drywall screws to do the job. Too often, these ordinary fasteners would pop up slightly after being pounded or driven into the concrete board. Water would then find its way to the popped-up head, and the screw or nail would begin to rust. This is bad for a couple of reasons. First, the rust stains can work through both tile and grout. Worse, the rust itself can deteriorate the nail or screw to the point where it severs the connection to the wall. If nothing is holding the concrete board in place, then nothing is holding the tile wall or tile floor in place, either.

Rock-On is a screw that is coated with an epoxy-based polymer coating called Climacoat that provides protection against chipping and moisture and corrosion and, as a result, resists rust. In addition, the screw is self-capping, which means it has a larger head. When drilled into the wall, it sinks slightly below the surface of the concrete board, and won't pop back up. This screw eliminates most of the problems involved in attaching concrete board. Make sure that anyone attaching concrete board in your bathroom renovation is using it.

rushed back to the store to buy a can of off-white paint to cover it all up. Make this same mistake with tile, however, and you're going to be stuck with your results for a long time to come. I have become wary of extremes when it comes to surfaces you can't change—perhaps because I have built so many houses on spec. Since everyone should act like a seller when making major decisions about how to renovate their homes, a little wariness on everyone's part would probably be healthy.

With tiles, I've learned through the years that basic is best, but it doesn't have to be boring. One of the most popular stones is a type of Spanish marble called Crema Marfil. It's probably my favorite, and comes in a beautiful beige color that's veined with white, like mocha swirled with milk. I recently worked on a house where the entire bathroom was done in this stone, including the shower and a Jacuzzi. The whole thing could have appeared monotonous done in this same stone, but we were able to add some interesting variations to it. As always, a great deal can be done in terms of décor just by mixing and matching different textures of the same stone, without going overboard by adding too many contrasting varieties.

For the shower and around the tub, we used large 12-inch-square polished tiles on the walls. For the floor, we used the same stone in 4-inch squares. Before the floor tiles were installed, the tile installer gave them a bath in muriatic acid—not something you would want to try on your own—to remove the polished finish and make them less slippery. This process is called etching. They ended up with a matte finish that looked even more refined than stone with a honed surface. To create an interesting design, the installer took some of the polished 12-inch tiles and cut them on his diamond-bladed tile saw to create little 2-inch-square "dots," as he called them. He added these in a clipped-corner pattern on the floor, which created a beautiful highlight to a great-looking bathroom. Every tile had one corner clipped, so it created a less busy pattern in the floor. We didn't go wild with colors and contrasts—in fact, everything was beige. But it shows that a little creativity can result in an interesting tile design that doesn't scream to be noticed.

Mount Up!

The color and texture of tile is important to consider, since it's such a major component of any bathroom. But for the tile to be permanent, it has to be installed on the walls and on the floor in a way that will last. Too often, people—whether homeowners or the average contractors—don't take the care that's needed to see that tiles are mounted correctly. As a result, I have seen the most beautiful tiles in the world flop loose in a matter of months because they're not properly attached. These end up clattering loose as people step on them along the floor, and allow water to leak when attached to shower and tub surrounds. This won't happen, however, if you follow some important steps.

The key to permanence in tiling lies not so much in the kind of tiles you buy; any tile, by its very definition, will likely endure for the life of your home. Instead, success depends upon what lies underneath the tiles. In this case, the rule is simple: Never mount tiles directly to wood, and never mount them directly to plaster or drywall. Although I'm a big fan of wood—it is a resilient material that moves back and forth when stepped on—tiles that are set directly onto it will eventually work loose. Drywall and plaster present another problem: Though perfectly adequate surfaces for a wall, these do not stand up well to moisture. Tile an ordinary sheet of drywall in a shower surround, and within a few short months it will turn to a damp mash.

Let's look at floors first, to see how they should be han-

Screws, Not Nails

When attaching concrete board, I have seen some people try to use nails to hold the board in place. Although this does indeed appear to work well, the effect is only temporary. Over time, the nails will work loose from the studs in the wall or the wooden subfloor because of vibrations from daily use, and the tiled surface will start to crack. Screws are the only fasteners that should be used in this case, because they grab into the wood in a way that will never vibrate loose.

dled. In the past, tile floors were set in a thick, cement-based material called mudset. Many shower basins are still created this way, and it involves pouring a sand-and-cement mixture about two inches thick, to create a solid, nonmoving base for the tiles that follow. To accommodate the thickness of the 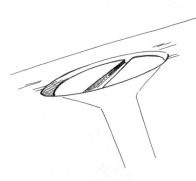 mudset floors, the other floors in the household had to be carefully calibrated in terms of height so that they would all match up. Except for the shower stall, this is an extravagant method that is rarely used today, although you will no doubt find remnants during a gut renovation of an old bathroom. Instead, there is a much better and cheaper method now available.

The solution today lies in concrete backer board (also known as cement board), which is sold under brand names such as Durarock, Wonder Board, HardiBacker, and PermaBase. This is similar to ordinary drywall used in walls and ceilings, with some important differences. For one, it's made of solid concrete that's held together with a Fiberglas mesh. The beauty of concrete for a bathroom lies in the fact that it withstands moisture, almost to a fault. In fact, I could take a piece of concrete board, throw it into Lake Michigan, and come back a month later and it would still have maintained its structural integrity. Ordinary drywall, by contrast, would turn to pulp within an hour. In addition, concrete expands and contracts only minimally compared to other materials, and is extremely stable as a result. Even as the wooden subfloor expands and contracts, the concrete board won't move—which means the tiles and grout will remain free of cracks. Under normal use in the bathroom, the concrete board will endure, even if the grout joint between the tiles cracks for some reason, or if the tiles begin to pull loose because they weren't correctly installed.

Concrete board comes in smaller sheets than drywall, with an average size of 3 by 5 feet, rather than 4 by 8 feet. This makes them easier to lift because, after all, they're solid concrete.

Installation of the concrete board requires great care, especially in how it is screwed into place. Rustproof screws, rather than nails, are essential; in addition, they have to be placed in a specific pattern rather than simply screwed in at random. For the floor, the screws should be placed every six inches around the perimeter of the room. Then, in the remaining area they should be screwed in place at regular intervals between 10 and 12 inches apart. You can get away with using fewer screws, but there is no guarantee the concrete board will be firmly attached to the subfloor—and you may see cracks form in the tile floor as a result. Pay attention as well to how the screws are driven into the board. They need to be countersunk, which means that the head of the screw lies below the surface of the board. There's literally a slight depression where the screw lies, so that if you drag a putty knife across the floor, it won't hit a single screw head. This will prevent the screws from popping up over time once the floor is finished, which could easily break or loosen the tile that is laid over it.

For walls, the task is somewhat simpler, since there is no subfloor involved. Instead, the concrete board is screwed directly to the wall framing, which is called the studs. You should install the screws every 6 inches along the edge of the material, and 8 inches in the field, or the center, of the board, to ensure a solid hold. The important part here is to make sure the edges of the board are screwed directly into the studs, even if this means cutting the concrete board into thin strips. This is the only way to guarantee a solid hold. While we're on the subject of cutting, let's discuss the best methods. An ordinary utility knife, which is the implement of choice for cutting drywall, works with concrete board, but the blade takes a beating. The object here is to score a line with the blade, then snap the concrete board along that line. A better method is to affix a small masonry blade to a circular saw and do the job that way. It cre-

Caulk Talk

As a material, grout is great to fill the gaps between tiles and make them watertight. But it's not for every area in the bathroom. Where the tile forms a joint with another material, whether it is the bathtub or shower surround, you need caulk instead. Although many people try to seal this area with grout, I don't recommend it, since there's too much movement as the different materials contract and expand. No grout, not even epoxy grout, can withstand this.

Instead, I prefer a silicone caulk for these areas. It stays flexible, compared to ordinary grout, and has the ability to withstand expansion and contraction of the surfaces it touches. The problem with ordinary caulk is its limited array of colors. You'll find clear, white, and—if you look hard enough—maybe black and almond, as well. Instead of a caulk line that blends into the tile line, you'll end up with a caulk line that looks more like an accent. An alternative is something called Polyseamseal, which is a latex product. But it has a more pronounced adhesive quality than regular latex, which makes it hold better. It also contains double the amount of mildewcide, which fights the growth of mold and mildew on the cured caulk surface. Because of its self-leveling features, it requires little or no tooling to achieve a nice, smooth bead. Better yet, it comes in more colors than you would want to know about, which gives you the ability to match just about any color tile—including cotton candy pink. The downside is that this latex caulk won't last as long as silicone caulk. While the joint between a tile floor and a bathtub might last five years caulked with silicone, you'll only get three years out of it with the latex version. Still, if looks and ease of installation are your concerns, this makes a great choice.

Dial "M" for Mortar

In general, I'm skeptical of suggesting do-it-yourself projects to homeowners. That's because, simple as these look on TV or in the how-to books, the reality is always much worse—and instead of a do-it-yourself project, it inevitably turns into an I-wish-someone-else-had-done-this project. A good example of this is tiling. Sure, it looks easy. You go to the home improvement store and come home with a few boxes of tiling, and you're good to go. Not quite. This is a profession—even an art. Yet since this also ranks as one of the most common projects that homeowners attempt themselves, I'm going to offer a few tips on how it can be done right.

The key to making tiles adhere to the floor or wall is to use something called thin-set mortar to hold them in place. This special mortar dates back to ancient Roman times and is still the best option today, with some modern additives. Tile setters attach the tiles piece by piece by spreading the thin-set on the back, combing it smooth with a notched trowel, then pressing the tile in place. This creates a good, level base that will hold tile or stone tight for ages.

To begin tiling—whether in a shower surround or on a bathroom floor—make sure that cement board panels have been used to line the area instead of ordinary drywall or plywood subflooring. Trowel a thin layer of mortar into the seams, where the panels meet. Then tape them with a 3-inch-wide Fiberglas mesh to seal the seams, and apply a thin layer over the top of that tape. This provides a waterproof surface that will hold the tile. Then, skim-coat every inch of panel with a layer of thin-set mortar.

ates a great deal of dust, but the cut comes out smoother as well as quicker. And, you're less likely to waste concrete board that crumbles instead of snaps just where you want it to.

Give a Shout for Grout

In a tiled surface, it's easy to overlook the crucial role played by grout. This, of course, is that very thin line of mortar that separates the tiles.

Mixing the mortar is the next step. A generation ago, tilers used ordinary portland cement for tiles, but this has little adhesive power. As a result, tiles would slide and move around until the material set. Modern ingredients such as finer sand and bond-enhancing additives make mortar far more tenacious today. When it's time to tile, you have to spread thin-set mortar on the wall or floor, as well as on the back of the tile. This "back buttering," as it is called, enhances the bonding ability of the mortar and helps the tiles go on flat so that they line up evenly with one another. After pushing a tile into place, twist it into the wall a bit to coax out air pockets that might weaken the bond. Then gently hit the center with a rubber mallet for a final fit.

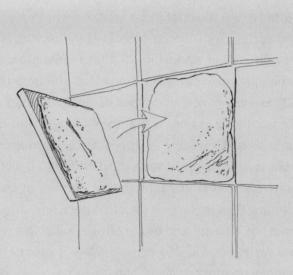

Sound simple? No—but if you're going to do it yourself, it's worth learning how to do it right. And make sure you practice on something other than the final surface.

What *is* its role, other than to fill the gap? Whereas tiles may be strong and durable, the grout that bridges the gap is designed to be flexible. With any settling or expansion, it is the grout—not the tiles—that should bear the brunt of the force and begin to crack. The grout also helps form a crucial layer of protection against water, which makes a tiled surface all but impervious to dampness.

Okay, so it's important—but all grout is the same, right? No way. As a result, choosing the right grout takes some effort, whether you're looking for grout to repatch an area, or whether you have to grout a freshly tiled surface for the first time. Luckily for you, choosing grout is not nearly as difficult as choosing the tiles themselves. That being said, there are some important considerations that will help the process along.

There are two major types of grout, known as sanded and unsanded. The unsanded variety is that thin line you find between perfect, machine-made tiles. It's chalky in appearance, no matter what the color. Sanded grout is literally grout with sand added to it as an aggregate. No surprise there. It's almost like a miniature version of concrete, and as such is far stronger than unsanded grout. Where unsanded grout is smooth, sanded grout has a rough and bumpy finish to it. Now, where would you use these two varieties? Sanded grout makes a great choice for floors, since the rougher texture creates a nonslip surface. Sanded grout is also the material of choice to use between rustic or handmade tiles, which have a slightly irregular shape. Where unsanded grout is more brittle and can only span a gap of ⅛ to ¼ of an inch without cracking, sanded grout can span a much thicker distance—easily a ½-inch or more—without cracking. Still, on walls, unsanded grout is preferable, because it has a smoother surface, which is more pleasing to the eye. Regardless, both types come in a profusion of colors; you can literally match or complement any type of tile with the choices available in any home improvement store.

Grout has been an unchanging element of tiling for thousands of years, but believe it or not, an improvement has been made in recent years. Will technology stop at

New Is Better Than Old

Although it's tempting to want to simply put new grout over old, don't. The two surfaces simply won't stick, and in no time things will look worse than before. Instead, you have to create a crevice or groove in the old material that gives the new grout an opportunity to grab hold and stick. By doing this, you'll have better-looking results that last.

nothing? You do have to wonder. The new technology is called epoxy grout, which has come into use in the last decade or so and is quickly gaining popularity for use in bathrooms. The best way to understand the advantages of epoxy grout is to pause and talk about the weaknesses of cement-based grouts. These types of grout are porous, especially the sanded varieties. They contain lots of pores and nooks to collect mildew and mold, and they absorb water just like concrete does. At the same time, the materials are inflexible. Any movement in the wall or floor will cause the grout to crack; surely, we've all seen examples of cracked grout in just about any bathroom we've ever been in. The epoxy grouts solve many of these problems. More related to synthetic rubber than to cement, they form a smooth surface that contains no pores whatsoever. This means mildew and mold can't get a toehold, even in the dampest of conditions. Since epoxy grout stays flexible, this creates a huge advantage in eliminating cracks and flaking grout.

The early versions of epoxy grout tended to be difficult to mix and apply, which caused this material to be relegated to the sidelines of the home improvement industry. But now, the major manufacturers of grout—including TEC, Henry, and Laticrete—make fabulous variations of epoxy grout. To be quite honest, I don't know why you would use anything else, other than the fact that it's slightly expensive. Whereas a bag of regular cement-based grout might cost $10, the same size bag of epoxy grout would cost about $50.

Epoxy grout will never stain from mold or mildew, but you do have to worry about one thing: It may stain the tiles that you're applying it to. Certain types of unglazed stone or rough-hewn tiles are porous, and will readily absorb the epoxy grout with no chance of being wiped clean. Ask at the tile store if a particular product can hold up to epoxy grout. If it can't, use cement-based grout instead. Or, consider choosing a different kind of tile. Also, keep in mind that you do have to work quickly with epoxy grout. Whereas applying cement-based grout can be a leisurely affair, with lots of time for lunch and other forms of procrastination, applying epoxy grout is

Don't Seal That Grout

Every time I flip through a homeowner's do-it-yourself magazine, it seems, I find another article about how to seal grout in a bathroom. The theory goes that by applying a liquid sealer onto these grout lines, you'll be able to block water penetration and also keep the grout from attracting dirt and becoming stained. I think this is a mistake, and I would never seal the grout in any bathroom, whether the tile is on the floor or in a tub or shower surround.

Sealing grout gives you a false sense of security in many ways. It creates the illusion that you're doing something to prevent mold and mildew, prolonging the life of the grout, and creating a maintenance-free surface. This is not the case, in my opinion. Applying sealers can actually trap dirt into the grout line, and can cause more problems than you had to begin with. In addition, the key to prolonging the life of the grout is to eliminate moisture problems in your bathroom, which are the source of most stains that develop. Although your grout might seem to hold up better with the sealer, you're missing an important clue as to the health of your bathroom's ventilation system—and you might pay for it by having far greater problems than a little bit of mildew to deal with.

How should you clean grout if it needs it? This is easy. There are countless products on the market that do the job by magic, but these are essentially nothing more than derivatives of bleach and water. A cheaper approach is to make your own concoction using about one part bleach to two parts water. Scrub the grout with the cleaner and an old toothbrush, and you'll restore it to its original color in no time.

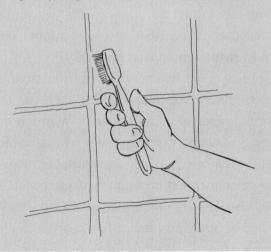

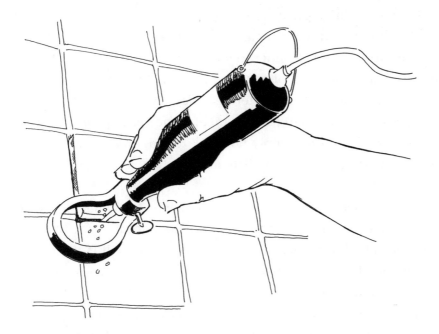

a race against the clock. You've got only about ten to fifteen minutes, and it's best to confine your work to a simple 4-by-4-foot area so that the grout doesn't harden in the middle of the task. Since you also have to wipe the tiles carefully so the grout doesn't adhere indelibly to the surface, I would definitely suggest that this be a two-person job.

Grout Reborn

If you're creating a brand-new bathroom, new tiling will inevitably be involved. But if you're doing a simpler renovation that does not involve new tiling, you can freshen up the look of an old tiled surface tremendously just by adding a new layer of grout. This is especially important if you're spending a lot of time and effort on other parts of your bathroom, such as new fixtures and cabinets, and the worn-out look of tiles becomes even more pronounced. Cleaning can only do so much; in many cases, you need to go in there and actually remove the old grout, and replace it with new.

Many people dream of quicker fixes to this problem. I have seen, for instance, "grout-painting kits" that purport to allow you to change the look of your bathroom simply with an artist's paintbrush. Save your money: It will not last longer than a few months. Others try to get by with the slapdash approach of applying grout to touch up areas where the old grout has fallen out. Or better yet, they try to slather a grout "veneer" over the top of the old grout to give it a newer appearance. This, too, is folly: New grout will simply not stick to old, and you'll end up wasting both your time and money. The only solution is to remove the old grout completely, then start over again.

When I mention grout removal, people instantly imagine kneeling for hours on end while they hand chisel the old grout away. True, this is one approach that has worked through the centuries. It is performed with a grout tool that literally resembles a toothbrush with a hard blade, which allows you to hand-scrape the old grout away. By the end of that project you'll not only vow never to do it again, but you'll either have tennis elbow or bursitis from all that scrubbing. A far better approach is to buy one of the most versatile power tools of all: a mini-rotary tool, such as those produced by Dremel. This handheld tool resembles a dental drill on steroids. And the company invented an attachment a few years ago specifically to help with grout removal.

This tool is held in your hand on a slight angle, almost like a gigantic pencil. The bit inserted in the end is then run up and down along the grout lines, where it literally just grinds them right out of the joints. You've got to be cautious, however, because the bit will also cut into the edges of the tile if you're not careful. Once you've finished with the tool, there is still a little bit of grout left that has to be removed by hand, but the task goes far quicker than the old-fashioned way.

Now that we've got the tile, plumbing, and ventilation systems in place, let's take a look at the core of the bathroom: the tubs, showers, toilets, and sinks, which give this room its purpose.

chapter FIVE

Fixated on Fixtures
Choosing tubs, toilets, sinks, and shower stalls can be bewildering; here's a road map.

Sometimes life presents too many choices, as my friend Lynn discovered when building a new home.

She and her husband made a deal with the builder: They would supply the fixtures in the bathroom in the hopes of saving a little money on the builder's markup. Fair enough. But what they saved in dollars cost a huge amount in aggravation, mostly because of the difficulty they had in making choices. Not just style and color, but types, and functions—from bathtubs with pliable headrests, to toilets with power-assisted flushing mechanisms. "When I couldn't make up my mind between the toilet described as having 'sleek, contemporary styling' and the one with '1890s ambiance,' I just about gave up," Lynn said. When the plumbers arrived to install the fixtures, they discovered that the items hadn't even been ordered yet, let alone delivered. "The next time I do this, I'm going to just pick a color—probably white—and let someone else make all the decisions for me," said the harried homeowner.

Shopping for fixtures can be the most difficult aspect of a bathroom renovation, because there are far too many choices. Take a look at toilets alone. You can have a one-piece toilet, a two-piece toilet, a low-flow flush

Go with the Low-Flow

As an engineering marvel, the toilet ranks among the world's greatest. There's the car, the electric lightbulb, and the toilet. Just try to imagine modern life without it. Toilets work because water leaving from the tank rushes into the bowl and creates a surge that carries waste over a barrier called a weir or dam and down the drain. Originally, tanks were placed high above the bowl to get water moving forcefully enough to clear the weir, but by 1915, narrower, smoother porcelain passageways allowed tanks to be mounted on the backs of bowls. One drawback, however, was that these toilets consumed a great deal of water, often 5 gallons or more with every flush. In 1994, federal law restricted new tanks to 1.6 gallons per flush, but this created additional problems at first, in that the toilets needed more than one flush to clear things out. Homeowners hated these, and many people will do anything to avoid them—including driving to Canada, where you can still buy the old-style toilets. The manufacturers have addressed this problem by further modifying the passageways to move a reduced amount of water more vigorously into the bowl.

No one should dismiss the water-savings potential in these fixtures. In New York City alone, the low-flow toilets save enough water to fill the equivalent of more than 2,000 Olympic-sized swimming pools each year. I think it's your duty, as a water-conserving American, to install them. So let's close the lid on this particular topic, once and for all.

toilet, or a low-flow, power-assisted flush toilet. You can have an elon-gated-seat toilet or a round-seat toilet. Then there are designer toilet pos-sibilities, including one from Japan that, I kid you not, has an electric heater installed to prewarm the toilet seat for you. I haven't even touched on the multitude of possibilities with regard to sinks, bathtubs, shower surrounds, and luxury items such as whirlpools, steam showers, and even bidets (as if anything used for what this is intended could be called "luxury").

These all come in enormous variations and with enormous differences in price. Yet, at the same time, they all look numbingly the same. You start to pore over the features of this toilet, or that soaking tub, or this sink, and that shower surround, and you begin to hallucinate at the choices. It's like saying the same word over and over again; before long, it becomes nothing but gibberish. As with my friend Lynn, this often leads to an inability to actually make selections. Unless you learn to manage the process, you'll never get your bathroom started, let alone finished, because you'll become so mired in all the choices that exist.

Let's work through each category of bathroom fixture to help narrow the field. Though I can't choose the fixtures for you, I can give you con-fidence to help you know when to call off the search and settle on some-thing. I'll also include some tips on installation. When you've finally

Plumbers Go Lightly

When bolting a toilet to the floor, use your fingers to set the bolts, then a small box wrench to tighten them gently. Notice that word "gently." If you lean into the wrench with all your weight, you'll risk cracking the base of the toilet. The bolts have nothing to do with whether the toilet leaks—that's the job of the wax ring. Instead, you're better off leaving the nuts a little looser and tightening them as the fixture settles over a few days than trying to tighten them once and for all.

poured in the energy needed to narrow down the choices, you'll need to make sure they're installed correctly—whether you're doing the job yourself, or having it done for you.

Things That Go Flush

What is striking about toilets, considering the singular purpose of their function, is the profusion of styles. Not just colors, but styles, shapes, and flush mechanisms. Function should come first, however, with fancy coming in second. Maybe plumbers should be faulted for not being interested in color and styling, but those aren't their primary concerns. Put simply: Get the toilet that does the best job.

Unlike other bathroom fixtures, toilets come in one material—namely, vitreous china. Fired at a very hot temperature, this is all but indestructible. Beyond this, toilets share something in common with women's bathing suits in that they come in both one-piece and two-piece varieties. The decision comes down to aesthetics, or as much aesthetics as there can be, considering you're talking about a toilet. A one-piece model is sleeker and often more contemporary in styling, and offers a lower profile that is less prominent. Put that behind a low divide at the end of a tub and it will disappear. These have a practical aspect, as well, in that they're easier to clean because there is no gap between the two pieces. The two-piece toilet, however, has a more familiar look, with a separate tank and

Elongated versus Round

Forget Coke versus Pepsi, Macs versus PCs, or even protein versus carbohydrates. The real debate in modern life centers on toilet shapes. In short, do you prefer round or elongated seats?

Let's look at this delicate topic in terms of style. Round ones have a cuter look to them, and seem more cozily at home in a bathroom. Elongated ones seem more like what you would find in a truck-stop rest room. So much for my discussion of toilet fashion. Instead, I think you should look at this from a practicality issue. Surprisingly, this is not so much a male versus female issue as it is one of size. If you're petite, round-seated toilets work great. If you're larger, then you'll appreciate the extra maneuvering room that the elongated seat can give you, regardless of your gender.

A final point: Round-seated toilets take up less space than their elongated siblings. If you have a miniscule powder room or a half bath and are trying to make the most of every square inch, this is the choice for you.

A No-Sweat Toilet

Picture a toilet in hot, humid weather. What do you notice? The outside of the toilet tank sweats harder than Andy Roddick at the U.S. Open. Here's why: The water in the tank is cooler than the air temperature, which causes any humidity in the air to condense on the outside of the tank. It accumulates, then drips to the floor, where it can cause a lot of damage over time. Old houses routinely have to have the floor structure rebuilt near the toilet, because of all those summertime dousings.

A solution for this is fairly straightforward, and involves a no-sweat kit available for about $10 from any plumbing supply center or well-stocked home improvement store. The kit contains pieces of Styrofoam insulation, which are easy to install. First, shut off the water supply to the toilet and then flush it, which will drain the tank and prevent it from refilling. Lifting the lid off the water tank, you literally line the inside of the tank with foam that is held in place with a silicone-based glue.

Fitted correctly, the foam lining insulates the tank and prevents the cold water from coming into direct contact with it. The result: no more dripping.

bowl, and is also available in a wide range of styles. One new option to consider for either type of toilet is a slightly higher seat, which is designed to meet the Americans with Disabilities Act's standards, and provides greater comfort to some users.

As the least glamorous task in home renovation, the installation of a toilet requires cautious care. Most people want to get it over with fast. But if you do it even the least bit wrong, you'll end up with a leaky mess. To replace a toilet, the crucial first step is to shut off the angle stop, which is the small water valve protruding from the wall below the tank. This keeps water from jetting all over you and all over the bathroom when you remove the toilet. After this, flush the toilet to empty it completely, then sponge out whatever little water might be remaining in the tank. When the water is turned off and emptied, the water supply tube connected to the toilet can be removed. If the toilet is a two-piece type, the two pieces have to be separated. To do this, remove the caps covering the bolts that hold the toilet together, and then unscrew the nuts. This is something that often requires more than a wrench, due to corrosion. I almost always find myself using a hacksaw, or at least penetrating oil, to loosen the nuts. When they're off, tilt the bowl forward to avoid spilling any residual water, and then remove it. With the toilet gone, you'll want to block up the drainpipe with a rag or large wad of newspaper to block any sewer odors while you're working.

The key to installing a new toilet correctly lies in making sure that it is well sealed where it connects to this drainpipe. To accomplish this, the toilet rests on a wax ring that fits around the drain. These wax rings are standard items sold in the plumbing section of any home improvement center. These wear down over time, so instead of reusing an old ring, always put a new one in place, then put the new bowl *gently* on top of it. The weight of the toilet compresses the seal for a very tight fit. With the

Did You Say Bidet?

I had a friend named Frank who ended up spending his junior year abroad in Paris. Lucky fellow, sort of. He loved everything about the place, he told me, including the fact that "they've got these nifty little basins right in the bathroom where you can wash all your laundry by hand." Yes, he was wringing out his socks and underwear right there in the bidet.

While wildly popular in Europe—in some countries such as France no well-equipped household is without them—bidets have been something of a curiosity in the United States, to say the least. I have installed exactly two in my career, but the tide does seem to be shifting. They are installed exactly like toilets, and privacy in using them is every bit as essential, if not more so. Increasingly, high-end designers are adding small compartments in luxury bathrooms to hold both a toilet and a bidet, which guarantees that what goes on there can be concealed by a door. While bidets are not exactly a trend—don't expect people to be wheeling them through the Home Depot checkout line anytime soon—they are becoming something of a fashion statement. Expect to see more of them appearing over the coming decade.

Now, if only we can figure out what to do with them.

toilet in place, gently (I know, this is an odd word to keep using when talking about toilets) tighten the nuts that bolt into the floor. After connecting the new water supply line, the toilet is ready to go.

Bathtubs

As with toilets, the range of styles and materials you'll come across when shopping for a bathtub is mind-boggling. Today, tubs run the range from boxy traditional designs to freestanding or soaking tubs, some of which rank as sculptures in their own right. Bathtubs, like preformed shower stalls, come in an assortment of modern materials such as acrylic, reinforced Fiberglas, and synthetic marble.

For my money, I prefer a traditional material for its durability: cast-iron enamel. It will hold up the longest, and can be refurbished if the surface ever wears out. True, they're heavy—you need three men and a boy to haul and lift them in place—but they'll last. This comes at a cost—anywhere from $350 to an astounding $5,500, which is the most expensive tub I've ever seen in a catalogue, but it's worth the money. One thing I would caution everyone against is a lightweight alternative called porcelain enamel steel. True, this may seem to have its appeal because it's far cheaper and far lighter than cast-iron enamel; it probably only takes a boy minus the three men to haul it in place. Yet even though it looks just like a cast-iron enamel tub when installed, it has an Achilles' heel: It's tinny sounding. When you step in it, it sounds just like you're stepping into a giant soda can. Worse, these tubs do not hold up for more than a few years. Because the tubs flex, the enamel begins to flake off and they begin to rust.

In most bathrooms, the tub acts simply as a focal

Get out Your Ruler

Remember, before buying any tub, carefully measure the doors and walls *en route* to the bathroom to be sure the unit fits through them. I learned this the hard way— after I had ordered and paid for a tub that never made it past the staircase.

Let's Talk Caulk

To prevent water leakage, bathtubs need to be caulked around the edge, where they come into contact with the floor and the bathtub surround. Make sure you caulk when the bathtub is filled with water and keep it full until the caulk has fully cured. Otherwise, the caulk will stretch and eventually pull loose as the bathtub fills with water.

point, while the day-to-day cleaning tends to be done in a separate shower. In addition, a well-designed shower is safer to use than many tub/shower combinations, mostly because these lack firm footing and adequate grab bars. Still, for appeal, and for the occasional long soak, nothing can be quite as satisfying. When fitted with a whirlpool kit, for instance, the effect of the bath can be sublime. Just don't expect to use it as much as you think. One of the most common complaints I hear from people is that they spent thousands of dollars to install a whirlpool tub, yet only use it once or twice a year. If you're going to use it, and can be sure of that, great; if not, spend your money elsewhere.

Since the bathtub is no longer used much for bathing, some designers have focused on a tub's soaking qualities. This tradition hearkens back both to Rome, where citizens gathered in public baths to exchange ideas, as well as to Japan, where it is believed that a quiet soak purges the body of impurities. Strictly speaking, a soaking tub is distinguished by its size. They are generally deeper than conventional tubs—up to 25 inches deep, compared to 15 inches—and are both larger and wider, as well. One downside is that this translates into a great deal of extra weight, since

Refinishing an Old Tub

Nothing fits the style of a bathroom better than a classic bathtub. Sadly, many of these have become rusted and pitted through years of drips, and scourings with harsh detergents. People very often rip out old tubs because they're slightly blemished. But it's not easy to find an affordable bathtub with the look and size of a period tub.

One solution is to have the old tub refinished through a process that involves coating it with an acrylic urethane resin coating. Done correctly, this is an effective and inexpensive solution for porcelain that is chipped or worn out, or for a tub with a color that has gone out of style. For an average cost ranging from $350 to $600, refinishers can make an antique fixture look brand-new. Professional refinishing can be a cost-efficient solution for that retro look.

The process involves cleaning the tub to remove the impurities that can hinder adhesion of the new finish, such as soap scum. Chips and scratches are filled with Fiberglas putty, then are sanded with coarse-grit paper. With the surface prepared, a bonding agent is daubed on, enabling the acrylic urethane enamel to adhere to the porcelain's glassy surface. When all is ready, the tub is sprayed with three coats of enamel paint, cured with a heat lamp, then sanded smooth with ultra-fine paper. Finished this way, the new surface should last about ten years before it needs another coat.

soaking tubs can weigh between 500 and 2,000 pounds when filled with water. You'll have cause for concern if your house is framed in wood with standard 2-by-8 joists; they will need to be larger. You would have to consult a structural engineer about ways to support and disperse a tub's weight, which may include bolstering existing joists with extra timbers, or installing a steel beam beneath the tub.

Showers

As I mentioned, while the centerpiece of many designer bathrooms is a soaking tub or a whirlpool bath, the reality is that most people head to the shower. Face it: In our fast-paced society, many people end up using a whirlpool bath infrequently—maybe during the holidays and on their anniversary. Other than that, they jump in the shower and, in a few minutes, relieve stress, get clean, and get on with life. Just what a shower can be depends upon the space and budget you have. Custom-built showers can resemble spas, with pulsing jets of water angling in from all sides, and even a separate generator that can send in plumes of restorative steam.

While I love tile shower surrounds of all types, many people choose to use preformed shower stalls, and shower/tub combinations in their bathrooms, and these can also work well—with a few caveats. First, shop by brand, since these are not commodities. A great shower stall by Kohler or American Standard or Jacuzzi will last a lot longer than anything churned out by the No-Name Shower Stall Company. Second, shop by material.

There are two major options in choosing materials: acrylic and Fiberglas. I strongly recommend acrylic as the superior choice. Acrylic has some wonderful properties. First of all, it tends to flex and return back to its original shape, like a trampoline. This means it will stand up to decades of stepping in and out of the shower. Second, the color runs throughout the material, which makes it a renewable surface. If it scratches or otherwise dings, it can be buffed smooth and waxed by a professional and look like new again. In this, it has a lot in common with solid-surface countertops such as Corian.

An Acrylic Solution

Instead of using paint, one way to completely make over a bathtub or shower stall is to use an acrylic liner. This is an expensive procedure that can cost from $2,500 to $3,000—but it is still cheaper than a complete renovation requiring new fixtures. It can give you the look and feel of brand-new fixtures without the expense of having to rip your bathroom apart to achieve it.

The process has to be done by a professional, and involves inserting an acrylic liner right on top of the old fixture. It fits like a glove, and can even be used to cover ceramic tiles on a wall, and is a great quick fix for ugly or outdated tiles. The liner is held in place by commercial-grade, double-sided tape, which bonds super-tight. The liner fits into the area, and is tucked in behind any faucets and drains so that none of the seams are visible. Around the edges it is caulked into place after being installed. It gives the illusion of a brand-new fixture and makes a perfect, modest-cost alternative to ripping everything apart and adding a new one. When installed by a professional, an acrylic liner should have a lifespan of at least a decade, and probably much longer.

There's one caution, however: I would not recommend putting an acrylic liner on top of ceramic wall tiles that are loose or that cover a wall where there are obvious signs of water damage. You would simply be trying to cover up a problem rather than correct it, which is never a smart approach when it comes to your home.

A Solid-Surface Shower Surround

Although I'm a big fan of acrylic, its colors can be limited. One alternative is to line the shower with a solid-surface material such as Corian. It is more expensive than acrylic (a shower surround might cost $2,000 to $2,500 in material alone), but it comes in a huge array of colors and styles. Best of all, it's practically indestructible.

In short, it really has no drawbacks other than limited color availability—namely white, off-white, and marbleized blends.

At first glance, Fiberglas seems to have much of the same appeal. It looks shiny and beautiful, and is in fact even more glamorous-looking than acrylic. After all, this is the material that gives a new sailboat its sexy glimmer in the water. In this case, however, beauty really is skin deep. Just beneath the glossy surface lie those fibrous bits of glass. If the surfaces get scratched or are gouged, that's what you'll be looking at for the rest of your shower's life. No amount of buffing will fix it; in fact, buffing will dull the finish and only make things worse. Also, Fiberglas doesn't have the trampoline effect of acrylic. It does indeed flex when you step on it, but it doesn't pop back with the same resiliency. Over a number of years, it can crack—leaving you with a shower stall that needs to be replaced.

Steam Showers

Let me tell you about my wife's cousin Dave, who is an electrician. Whereas other people treat themselves to a sports car or Caribbean cruise, Dave treated himself to a steam shower in the basement of his house, for which he spent a total of about $3,500. After work, he steps in there, turns the steam on, and watches a day's worth of tension disappear into the mist.

Although traditional hot air saunas—the kind that are lined with wood, where you sit with a towel over your face—are a luxury beyond the reach of most people, a steam shower is something different. It can be fitted into an existing shower stall, and easily incorporated into a larger one during a bathroom renovation. When in operation, a small but powerful electric steam generator heats water from a dedicated supply line, then sends plumes of relaxing and head-clearing steam into the shower stall through one or more nozzles located near the floor. If I have a client trying to decide between a whirlpool or a steam shower, I recommend the steam shower every time.

In addition to the generator, construction of a steam shower requires a stall enclosure that is completely sealed off from the bathroom so all that steam cannot escape. Otherwise it'll peel the wallpaper off the entire top floor of your house. Shower curtains are useless in this respect; a tightly fitting floor-to-ceiling glass door is the only solution. Locating the generator can also require some maneuvering. Although only the size of a carry-on suitcase, it requires additional space to keep hot pipes away from wood framing, and an enclosure that can be accessed in case a part needs replacing. Generally they are put in a closet that abuts the shower area, or down in the basement—but the closer the better. To get the most steam, you want the most direct and short a pipe run as possible from the generator to the shower, with a maximum distance of 50 feet. The cost of these units is between $900 and $1,500—but the cost escalates, depending on how they're installed, as Cousin Dave discovered.

A Heavy-Duty Vent

With a steam shower, you're creating the equivalent of a science experiment similar to those that try to re-create the origins of life on Earth. This is fine, as long as you're actually in the shower, but the health of your bathroom and of yourself requires all that moisture be vented away the second you're finished. To do this, you need to have a second exhaust fan installed right into the steam shower area to handle the overload. An ordinary bathroom fan simply won't be up to the task.

Sinks

Broadly defined, sinks come in a number of categories that relate to their shape: counter-mounted, wall-mounted, and pedestal. In the bathroom, counter- or deck-mounted sinks remain the most popular. One advantage is that the counter they are paired with then provides plenty of shelf space for soap dishes, toothbrushes, hairbrushes, cosmetics, razors, and the collection of items that makes its way into the average bathroom. No one has enough storage space in the bathroom, which is why people tend to use the top of the water tank on the toilet for storage. And that's a bad idea, because what's on the toilet eventually tends to fall *into* the toilet. Counter sinks are the most popular to pair with a vanity, and can be fitted into any type of cabinet—whether stock, custom, or even antique.

Pedestal sinks have made a comeback in recent years, and offer a wide range of styles and designs. Some even have wide, flat tops that give you the equivalent of a small countertop around the edge. These pedestal sinks, which typically are made of vitreous china—the same material used in toilet construction—have two disadvantages: They offer little in the way of storage beneath them the way a counter-mounted sink does. And the plumbing that connects to them is not always invisible. Wall-mounted sinks are also enjoying a comeback. Connected to the wall with hangers or angle brackets for support, they are among the least expensive and the most compact sink options available. Proper connection to the wall is crucial. You usually

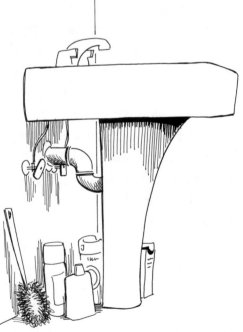

When Is a Sink Not a Sink?

Bathroom sinks, for reasons that have to do with Latin, are referred to as "lavatories" by most designers—which is a word that most of us stopped using in grade school. Though I don't want you to start reusing this term, I do want you to be prepared to encounter it when researching catalogues and talking to designers.

have to add a strip of wood to the wall, called a support ledger, to carry solidly the weight of the sink. This board is then covered with drywall or plaster before the sink is mounted in place.

A bathroom sink, like the old Model-T, used to come in whatever color a homeowner wanted—as long as it was white. In today's style-conscious world, however, the sink has become more of a fashion statement, and is now available in a multitude of styles and designs, sizes, and colors. Manufacturers coordinate sinks with a line of bathtubs and toilets, but bathroom renovators should feel free to mix and match at will. Often, these coordinating "lines" are just somebody else's idea of what looks good together. I think it's more essential for the faucets, towel racks, and other hardware to match, rather than the sink, tub, and shower.

Sinks come in a broad range of materials. The most durable is enameled cast iron, which is heavier than vitreous china or enameled steel. Fiberglas is lightweight for easier installation and is moderately priced, but tends to scratch and dull easier. And although an enameled steel surface is easy to clean and lighter and less expensive than vitreous china or enameled cast iron, it is also much less durable. For my money, I would go with enameled cast iron every time. There are also less-expensive sinks made from synthetic materials, such as "cultured marble," which work well because the sink and countertop are installed as one integrated piece. Solid-surface sinks and countertops, similar to those found in kitchens, are also making an appearance in the bathroom. They are not cheap, but they do offer the advantage of being practically indestructible. Specialty materials have also made an appearance, particularly in smaller powder rooms, where they lend a more formal or stylish look. These include sinks made from brass, copper, and even wood. But be careful in choosing these, because they require a lot of special maintenance; in most cases, sinks made with unusual materials work best as a focal point in a seldom-used guest bathroom or a powder room.

Faucets

Just as sinks have evolved, faucets are also now available in a profusion of styles to match them. The outward style may vary from faucet to faucet, but the quality of construction should not. What matters most is what the faucet is built of on the inside, rather than what it looks like on the outside.

Although a faucet might be plated in chrome, brass, or nickel, the fittings beneath are made of another material. In every case, you should choose solid-brass workings, because they hold up. Anything else, especially plastic, will deteriorate quickly. One simple way to determine what a faucet is built with is to pick one up in a store. The heavier, the better—a sure sign of the presence of mighty brass. In addition, the water-stopping mechanism inside a faucet is also an important consideration. The earliest

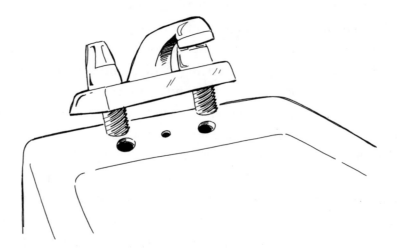

ones contained a valve fitted with a long screw called the stem. Turning the handle would grind a rubber washer into the valve's seat, and stop the flow of water. If you overtightened this kind of faucet, the washer would wear away and begin to leak.

As a remedy, manufacturers developed valves that opened and closed with a quarter-turn of the handle. These preserved the life of the rubber washer, but new technology has eliminated the rotating washers altogether. New, washerless valves have a stainless-steel cylinder encased in a plastic cylinder. As the handle turns, the cylinder holes line up and water flows. An even better system relies on a pair of super-smooth, super-hard ceramic disks that rotate against each other. Water streams out when the holes are uncovered, but can't get past any spot where the pieces touch. These valves can last forever.

Worn-out faucets can be replaced as long as the tailpieces of the new faucet fit exactly through the mounting holes of the existing sink or countertop. These are the cylindrical pieces that extend below the sink and connect to the water supply lines. Typically, faucets come in three very common sizes: single-holed faucets, in which both the hot and cold supply lines come through the same opening, and those with either a 4-inch or an 8-inch spread, which is a measure of the distance between the centers of the cold water and the hot water valves. The diameter of the holes can also vary, especially on old lavatories with tiny holes that do not correspond to the dimensions of modern faucets. The way to make sure the

Faucets to Last

Faucet finishes can corrode and become nicked during use, which deteriorates the finish. One solution is a process called particle vapor deposition, or PVD, in which vaporized metals are actually implanted into the fixture's skin. The resulting finish, such as a brass one, is invulnerable to scratching or corrosion. Still, never pour on the bleach or scouring powder to scrub up a faucet. Nothing is indestructible, so treat them right.

faucet you're buying will fit your sink is to measure the holes first, before you go to the faucet dealer. That way, you won't have to exchange the faucet when it doesn't fit—and be charged a needless restocking fee.

The hardest part of the task is to remove the old faucet. First, turn off and disconnect the water supply lines. This is an amazingly obvious step, but you wouldn't believe the number of people who forget it—and end up facing a geyser. If the nuts holding the faucet are corroded into place, spray on a penetrating oil to loosen them, or heat them delicately for a few seconds with a propane torch. Be careful, however, since some faucets may be made from chrome-plated plastic and will literally melt when hit with a blowtorch (which is one reason why I recommend avoiding them in the first place). Then use a basin wrench, which is a long-handled tool that can maneuver in tight areas, to remove the nuts that hold the faucet in place from beneath the sink. One precaution: When replacing a faucet, always add new supply tubes that connect the supply pipes to the tailpiece of the faucet. Old ones wear out, and there's no point in going through this effort only to have them spring a leak when you're all done. I prefer chrome-plated brass tubes to flexible plastic ones, because they have a longer track record in the industry. The plastic ones have all the structural integrity of a soda straw.

Now that we've gotten a handle on faucets as well as all the other fixtures, let's turn to one last yet crucial element of a bathroom—which is where to find places to put everything, from toothbrushes to towels.

Gentle Fingers

Adding a new sink, and especially a new faucet, is an exercise in finesse. It requires a couple of crescent wrenches (no pliers, please) and a light touch. Everyone tries to play King Kong and tighten the nut until the threads strip.

chapter SIX

A Place for Everything
Clutter ranks as the bathroom's defining problem; here's how to tame it.

Sometimes, the important part of a room is not so much what's in plain sight, but rather what's cleverly organized and hidden just out of view. Keeping it hidden, however, can be a monumental task, especially in a bathroom.

Acquaintances of mine, Jason and Terri, discovered this for themselves during a bathroom renovation. With about $15,000 in savings, they went for an extensive makeover that included ripping everything down to the studs and adding new sinks and faucets, a new tub, and new tiling. But when the costs started exceeding their budget, they had to make a choice between expensive marble tiles and a custom-made cherry vanity, or built-in storage space that would include a linen closet and additional cabinets. As if playing some home renovators' version of *Let's Make a Deal,* they opted for the fancier materials, which left little for storage. No built-ins, no closet squeezed into an unexpected space, and only one medicine cabinet they thought they could share. The vanity did seem to have space, but the top part of it was taken up with the sink, and the bottom part left little room. "We can always add these things later," Jason said, and the finished bathroom did look good—for about a week. Soon, things started piling up. The wastepaper basket was mounded high, and the tiny counter-top on the vanity became crowded with Jason's electric razor and collection of colognes, and Terri's creams and emollients. The medicine cabinet was so stuffed, it barely closed, and the whole place looked like a monument to toilet paper, which the couple would buy in bulk. "All right, we made a mistake," said Jason. "Storage is one of those things that you need to consider first, not last, in order to make a bathroom work."

Finding proper storage space in the bathroom is one of the most difficult things, mostly because of the tight quarters. In a kitchen, by contrast, you usually have plenty of space to work with, as with bedrooms, an attic, a basement, and even a living room. But in the bathroom, everything tends to be a microcosm. Make a list of the things you want in a

The Geometry of Mirrors

In a bathroom, you may want to have large, wall-sized mirrors that rise right up to the ceiling, and extend to the corner of the wall. They can make a bathroom feel much more voluminous and look great, as long as the person installing them pays attention to a few details.

The problem, as I see it, is that few walls and ceilings are perfectly straight, and even fewer of them form right angles where they meet. Instead, carpentry is a sort of big-picture affair, with lots of deviations in any particular detail. Many times, mirror installers make a template based on these imperfections, and cut the mirror to match the wall. If they do this, you might end up with a mirror that looks more like a parallelogram. Or, if you have a mirror with a curved top, you'll end up with gentle undulations to match the space. While this is a noble effort on the part of the installer, the results are botched. Your eye is trained to follow the edge of the mirror, and this technique will accentuate the differences rather than mask them.

Instead, cut the mirrors to the shape you want: squares, rectangles, arcs—you name it. Then, have the carpenters follow up with a little plaster to make the ceiling and the walls line up with the edges of the mirror. The imperfections will fade away, and you'll be left with a dazzling impression.

bathroom, and it's enough to fill an entire store. Towels and washcloths. All that toothpaste, hair gel, dental floss, and baby powder you got on sale. A six-month supply of toilet paper. A stack of magazines. And the endless array of hairbrushes, curling irons, hair dryers, bathrobes, slippers, wet towels, dry towels, shampoos, and conditioners. You'd need an entire warehouse just to store all this stuff, and somehow we expect it all to vanish neatly into a 5-by-7-foot room. Add a couple of children elbowing each other for sink space, or a working couple both trying to catch the morning bus, and you've got chaos in the making.

What's needed is a giant compactor. Don't despair, however. There are intelligent ways that you can make everything fit, as long as you don't wait until the tiler leaves to start thinking about it. Let's take a look at storage, and figure out how to make the most of it in this tiniest of rooms.

Vanity Fair

For years, the bathroom was nothing but the most utilitarian room in the house. Yet while the fundamental purpose has remained the same, the surroundings have definitely been elevated, especially with the addition of fine-looking cabinetry known as vanities. Incorporating these in styles you love takes the bathroom beyond the sterile, plain room it once was.

Vanities can be as diverse as anyone's imagination allows them to be. Architects, for instance, create washstands from scratch. In addition, ready-made cabinets can be customized by adding legs or drawers in addition to the sink. For those who want a more distinctive look, vintage bureaus or cabinets bought from antiques shops or yard sales can be fitted with a sink and a countertop and put into service. Faucets for vanities can be built directly onto the countertop in the traditional way, but manufacturers are now building wall-mounted versions that free up this space entirely.

The standard vanity depth is 21 inches. But you can gain floor space in a small bath by trimming at least part of the vanity to 18, 15, or even 12 inches deep—and still end up with useable space. You might also add a wider countertop that extends to the wall beyond the edge of the vanity, or that might even extend over the back of the toilet. This is typically called a banjo top because its shape is wider at one end toward the sink, then narrows like the neck of a banjo over the toilet. If you're using a

Vanities without Vanity

Look in any designer magazine and you'll find bathroom vanities built like furniture, which make even high-quality kitchen cabinets feel lowly. Although these have great appeal with respect to style, they don't necessarily rank high on the practicality meter. Even if your bathroom has no humidity or ventilation problems (which it won't, if you've read and followed Chapter 2), bathroom cabinets are still subject to splashes when you jump out of the shower, and drips when you brush your teeth. Adults can usually find a way to do these activities neatly, to preserve the cabinets, but children often can't. In this case, I'd recommend a vanity surface called Thermofoil.

Vanities made from this material are actually constructed of medium-density fiberboard, or MDF. The surfaces are then coated with thermal foil, which is literally a thick plastic coating that is "heat shrunk" in place. The result is a surface that's durable, easy to keep clean, and very inexpensive. For a family bathroom, it's ideal. True, you may not get the beauty of hand-burnished bird's-eye maple, but you'll be getting a good product at an even better price that will hold up for decades. Now *that's* beauty.

banjo top, be sure you either hinge the section over the toilet tank so it lifts for repairs or use a one-piece, low-profile toilet. You might also find the 30- or 32-inch standard height of a vanity too low. If so, consider building up the toe kick on a stock vanity or ordering a taller one that stands 34 to 36 inches off the floor.

Despite the trend toward exotic vanities that can be seen in house magazines, most of us seem to be relegated to the small bathroom with your typical sink base/vanity. This really is very similar to the sink cabinet in the kitchen, and though it can be attractive, it does not offer huge volumes of space. Instead, it's typically just a cabinet below, with the space taken up largely by plumbing. One smart way to add space is to choose a vanity with drawer storage instead of doors. Most items stored

in a bathroom are small and get lost at the bottom of a cabinet or on shelves. Drawers can be made even more efficient with molded-plastic dividers and cosmetic trays. You can even consider narrow rollout shelves on either side of the P-trap under the sink; just get in the habit of storing cleaning supplies elsewhere—like in the linen closet out in the hallway, where you can find them on cleaning day.

One way to make space for drawers in a small vanity cabinet is to put the plumbing to one side so you can get one-half of it lined with drawers, even if the other half is a cabinet door that contains the plumbing inside. You might only end up with three small drawers in the cabinet—but that's three precious drawers' worth of space that otherwise would be absent. A 30-inch sink base with a cabinet door might cost $100, and upgrading to one with drawers might cost $150.

But this will be the best $50 you'll ever spend, and probably the easiest way to get a little extra storage space in your bathroom without changing the configuration.

With a larger space to work with, the combination of cabinets and storage areas can be endless. You can find vanity bases spanning 6 feet and longer, and available in almost every configuration. A center sink base, with drawers both to the left and to the right, will span about 5 feet of space, and give you a tremendous storage potential. With this much space, it's possible to create a little knee space beneath the countertop, which makes it convenient for someone to sit down and apply makeup, and also offers a place to tuck the wastepaper basket.

One Sink, Two Sinks

If you've always wanted a double-bowl vanity, think twice. Two bowls are useless if two people don't have enough elbow room to use them at the same time. You'll need at least 60 inches from side to side—72 inches, if possible.

An R_X for Storage

Years ago if you heard the word "medicine cabinet," something not so pleasant would come to mind: a wall-mounted box, with a mirror and dingy metal. It not only held medicine, it looked medicinal, too—like it was a leftover from some hospital surplus sale.

Fortunately, medicine cabinets have come a long way, to the point where they're now architecturally pleasing. You can find them with mirrored fronts, with the advantage of hidden space behind it. Most cabinet manufacturers also make wooden ones so that you can literally match your vanity and your medicine cabinet for a polished, put-together look. The rules for shopping for these are the same as for shopping for cabinets and vanities: Look for brand-name manufacturers such as Wood-Mode, Brookhaven, Omega, and Decora, as well as

A Well-Insulated Medicine Cabinet

If a medicine cabinet is set into an exterior wall—that is, one that faces the outside of a house—it needs to be carefully insulated to avoid freezing the Pepto-Bismol in cold climates. First, the wall behind the cabinet should be insulated with ½-inch-thick rigid foam insulation, or however much Fiberglas insulation will fit before the cabinet is installed. Then, once it's set in place, the gap around the cabinet should be tightly caulked to prevent drafts.

others. These manufacturers also produce medicine cabinets in an array of shapes, including corner models, that can help you take advantage of underused space in the bathroom.

Medicine cabinets can be installed in a couple of ways, and the best way—if you're working on an extensive bathroom renovation where you go down to the studs—is to build it into the wall. Medicine cabinets are typically set about 3½ inches deep into the wall, which corresponds to the depth of most wall framing. This gives them a built-in look, as if they were always intended to be built in rather than hung on the wall as an afterthought. If you can't recess them into the wall, whether because plumbing and wiring have already taken up the space or because your renovation is not that extensive, it is still possible to get a built-in look by mounting the medicine cabinet directly on the surface of the wall. If the vanity cabinet fills a small nook—say, between the wall and the end of the bathtub—there may be just enough space in the wall to fit a medicine cabinet. Since you can't view the cabinet from the side, it will have the appearance of being built into place.

Closet Desires

For many people, having a bathroom closet ranks as one of those unattainable fantasies—like becoming a concert pianist, or learning to ice-skate backward. If you've got a bathroom with a great deal of space, read

Storage to Go

Bathroom designers pride themselves on being able to outfit a room with beautiful built-in vanities and storage areas. But one of the realities for homeowners is that they have to find storage after the fact—that is, after the bathroom has already been built, or as a low-cost addition to a basic bathroom makeover. Fortunately, many companies sell ready-to-install bathroom storage cabinets, such as those designed to straddle the toilet, and rise up above it to include three or four shelves for towels and other bathroom paraphernalia, from curling irons to toilet paper.

One thing to be mindful of is the quality of the storage units. It's difficult to gauge this if you're buying it online or through a catalogue. Instead, I think it's worth a visit to see it firsthand in a store. While there, spend a little time with it—not enough to make a nuisance of yourself, but enough to give it a good test-drive. Open and close the drawers and cabinet doors a dozen or more times to get a sense of how they'll hold up. Pay attention to the tactile qualities so you'll know how it feels, rather than just how it looks. There's usually a price range for these units, from those on the bargain end to those that are slightly more expensive.

Choose these correctly, and they'll not only become a functional aspect of your bathroom in terms of storage, they'll become an aesthetic enhancement, as well.

no further. You're lucky, and can make the most of it. But even if you have a pinched and cramped little room to work with, the chances are good that you can locate a few square feet with which to build some useful storage. You may not be able to load it full of coats and boots, but you'll at least find space for some towels and a fraction of the bathroom's necessities.

The key to finding space is to look behind the walls, which can easily be accomplished during a major renovation. Many times, especially in older homes, the walls are filled with gaps called chases that were built to carry the plumbing, heating, and electrical systems. These were usually built with room to spare. And you can sometimes steal this space for a new storage area. These gaps become more apparent when you're doing a gut rehab, because you tend to see the stud space—as well as with new construction, where you may notice areas where the furnace ducts, the plumbing waste stack, or the water pipes rise into the rooms. Most builders, who think only in terms of large areas, tend to ignore these little pockets, but you, the average storage-hungry homeowner, can easily spot them. Just imagine what you could fit into an area 8 inches wide by 8 feet tall! If the space is wide enough, it can be fitted with a door and turned into an actual closet; if not, it

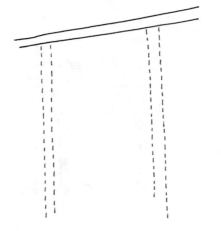
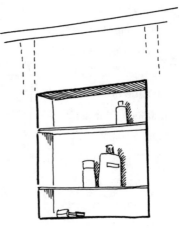

A Nice Niche

One of the most clever ways to create a little extra space in a bathroom is to add a narrow set of shelves right between the studs. To do this, you build an indentation that's about 3 feet tall and 3½ inches deep, line it with drywall, and fill it with two or three glass or wooden shelves. This niche makes a great spot for colognes and perfumes, as well as the occasional small vase of fresh flowers. Best yet, it takes advantage of "real estate" already in your bathroom that would otherwise go unused. One note: If you install this niche into an exterior wall,

insulation is essential. Instead of adding drywall to the back, add a ½-inch-thick piece of rigid foam board. Then cover this with a thin layer of plaster or joint compound before painting or wallpapering.

can simply be left as open shelves. Either way, it's free space, and yours for the taking.

Another way to create some additional space in this manner is to reorient the fixtures that you're using, or to choose smaller fixtures specifically to create additional nooks. Consider turning the bathtub a quarter-turn, and perhaps by reorienting it in this way you may create a dead space for a closet or a row of shelves. Working on a rental apartment building some years ago, I tried this out to good effect. The units had bathtubs in these miniscule 5-by-6-foot bathrooms, but I found that by putting in a 3-foot shower surround instead of a 5-foot bathtub I was

Talking Trash

You can spend thousands of dollars on a bathroom renovation, but the sad truth is that if you haven't sorted out in advance where to put the wastepaper basket, you're going to end up with an eyesore right in the middle of your newly tiled room. You can try to cover this up by getting some artsy, handpainted wastepaper basket, but within a day or two it's going to become heaped with tissues and dental floss and cardboard toilet paper rolls and cotton swabs, and will look more like Oscar the Grouch's lair. Instead, trash needs to be managed. Just as you think out where you're going to take a bath, and where you're going to hang your towel to dry, ask where the obvious spot for the wastepaper basket should be. In my bathroom, the countertop extends over the vanity cabinet by about a foot and a half, which gives us just enough space to tuck in the wastepaper basket. If you find a place for the trash beforehand, you won't end up staring at it after your bathroom is finished.

able to create an opening for shelving. It was the kind of detail that nobody could have predicted when drawing up the plans, but it became possible to visualize once we got into the bathroom and started to work. Instead of drywalling this up as dead space, we knocked a couple of studs out, drywalled the indentation, and put in shelves and painted them. Now every tenant uses them for towels and supplies. We also made use of an additional gap by the sink. The vanity cabinet was a standard 30-inch-wide variety, but it stopped nearly a foot away from the wall. Instead of ignoring the space, I put a longer countertop over the cabinet base that reached all the way to the wall. Not only did this give people more working area by the sink, it also created a nice gap beneath it to hide the wastepaper basket.

During a renovation, just look for ways to maximize the use of space and you will be guaranteed to find storage space—even in the smallest of rooms.

Clothes Call

House hunting with my wife, Mary Beth, one day some years ago, we found ourselves numb from looking at so many places. Some were beauties, others not at all, but one house stood out among the rest. And the reason? It had an old-fashioned laundry chute, used for sliding dirty clothes from the upstairs bathroom all the way down to the washing machine in the basement. "I've always wanted a house with a laundry chute," she confessed. "This is the one for me." And so we bought it. Houses are funny in this way. Sometimes it's the unexpected aspects that stand out, and that shape how you view the whole place. I can't guarantee that adding a laundry chute will help you sell your house some day, but I can guarantee that it will make your life much more convenient while you live there. Whoever is in charge of the laundry in your house is going to thank you every day—or at least every laundry day.

A Chute for All

Since laundry chutes have to run straight downstairs, it's not possible to link them up to more than one bathroom on the same floor—unless they're adjacent.

If you want the laundry chute to service more than the bathroom, a solution would be to find a central laundry chute opening in a main hallway for everyone to use, rather than to locate it in a single bathroom. In my old house, the laundry chute was located at the top of the stairs, and passed through the kitchen on the way to the basement—so we could also feed it full of towels and dishrags.

A Hamper for All

As much as I'm a big fan of laundry chutes, they're not for everyone, especially for those with a laundry room upstairs near the bedrooms rather than downstairs where it can be reached by gravity. In these cases, I recommend a hamper that is built into the vanity cabinets, much the same way a trashcan can be built into a kitchen cabinet. These hampers are covered with the same door front as the vanity cabinet, except that the door tilts open to reveal the hamper. You put dirty clothes in, push the door shut, and you won't have to see or think about them again until washday. These hamper cabinets should be a decent size. The smallest one that I've seen work was about 15 inches wide and 24 inches deep (although it could just as easily work with those measurements flipped). These work well in a master bathroom, but they make the biggest impact on a household when installed in a children's bath: Give them a place to put their laundry and they will be more likely to use it, which helps both them and you stay organized.

Laundry chutes are surprisingly easy to install, especially if you're doing a gut renovation of a bathroom and exposing the wall framing. In the old days, these chutes were built out of metal ductwork, similar to that used in forced–air heating systems. While durable, metal ducts are not the best material for this because they contain tiny ridges where the various pieces fit together. Occasionally, this ridge will snag a pair of jeans or a shirt, and require you to fish around for it with an unbent coat hanger. What works far better than this is a concrete form called a Sonotube. This resembles a giant paper towel roll and is used for pouring footings for decks. It comes in different lengths and can be pieced together easily in the wall. An alternative is plastic culvert pipe, which fits together with joints like metal ductwork, but the ridges inside are smooth—which means the risk of snagging clothes is minimal.

In order to get them right, these chutes come with a few rules. First, you never want to have a laundry chute that's flush with the floor in the bathroom. The risk is too great that children or pets could some-how open them up and fall into them. Instead, they should be located with the opening about 24 to 30 inches off the floor, and covered with a door. Something that matches the vanity would be ideal. The tubes themselves should be about 14 inches in diameter if you're using a round one, or 10 inches on each side if you're using a square one. The opening in the bathroom can actually be smaller than this, however, which serves two purposes. First, it prevents someone from actually trying to climb in it, and second, it forces you to put clothes in one arti-cle or two at a time, which will reduce the risk of jamming the tube by trying to stuff too much in at once.

There is one limitation, however. Laundry chutes have to be built in a straight up-and-down run, except for the 90-degree turn that opens into the bathroom. If you try to put a few curves and kinks in them, perhaps to connect to another bathroom, you'll end up with a chute full of clothes faster than you can say, "Why did I ever build this thing?" The tube should run through the walls straight down into the basement. There, it can either open in the basement ceiling and spill onto the floor near the washing machine, or you can have it empty into a big laundry basket down there, perhaps one that is set into a cabinet if you have a finished area.

Quite a few new homes I have worked on recently have a different setup altogether. In these houses, the laundry is located on the second floor, not in the basement or on the first floor. Laundry chutes clearly would not be of any help here, but who knows? Maybe this will resurrect another old-fashioned device: the dumb waiter, which could be used to haul dirty clothes up to the second floor.

Hang It All

Beyond vanities and conventional closet space, the bathroom contains plenty of possibilities for storage in the form of shelves and racks that attach directly to the wall. These include toilet paper dispensers, towel racks, clothes hooks, and shelves for knickknacks that can also hold a tremendous volume of bathroom items.

Open shelving is probably the single best way of adding more storage potential to a room, especially because of the shelving possibilities that exist. It's easy to find glass shelves that hold securely to the wall with

A Warm Idea

One of the niftier trends in bath design is towel warmers rather than towel racks. These literally act like a radiator and heat up; and they not only warm the towels and help them dry faster but also give you a good source of supplemental heat. If you have hot water heat, the piping can literally be extended right through the specially designed warmers. Electric units also exist, for those with other heating systems. Either way, these units are a true luxury that cost anywhere from $500 to $1,000 and even more—but they're a luxury you'll be grateful for every wintry day.

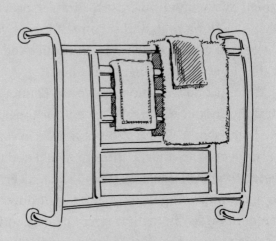

two small pieces of hardware, and just a screw or two. The beauty of a glass shelf in the bathroom is that, because it's transparent, it doesn't feel as though you're shrinking the space of the bathroom by installing it—because you can see through the glass itself. At the same time, these shelves can hold a bundle. You can roll your towels and stack them like

---

Getting Hooked

Towel bars work great for normal-sized towels. But the trend now is for "bath sheets," which are jumbo-sized towels. Trying to fold one of these up to squeeze onto the typical towel bar could rank as an Olympic sport. A better solution is to install hooks; the towels will drape easily on these, and have a much better chance of drying out.

---

logs in a woodpile. You can line up the rolls of toilet paper, or use them next to the vanity to hold perfume bottles or even an ever-changing display of fresh flowers (who said I didn't have a flair for home décor?). Form and function work together with these shelves, and I have seen them in catalogues and bath stores for as little as $15—which surely ranks as one of the greatest bargains in home improvement.

For metal towel racks and toilet paper dispensers, I take the same approach in choosing these as I do in choosing doorknobs: Shop by weight, which is a sign that they're made with solid brass rather than plastic just beneath the surface layer of chrome or other metallic finish. You can go to a home center and buy a cheap three-piece set that includes an 18-inch towel bar, a 15-inch towel bar, and a toilet paper dispenser. Then, you can pick up a single 15-inch towel bar made by a good brand such as Baldwin or Jado, and it will weigh more than the entire box of three combined. Your mind may ask you, "Why do I care how solid a towel bar is, as long as it's mounted on the wall?" But, believe me, you'll know the difference. Not only can you literally feel the difference when you go to hang up a towel, but the finish will hold up for a lifetime. If you're installing ceramic towel racks and toilet paper holders, keep

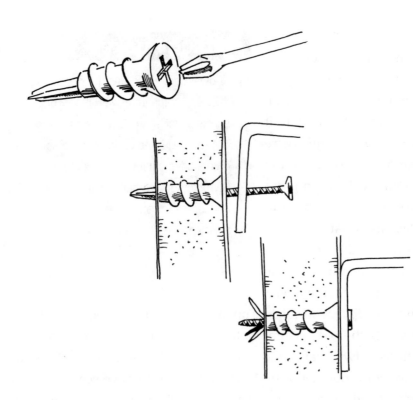

your eye on quality, as well. Here, you'll need to examine the finish to make sure that the entire visible surface is properly glazed. Any cracking in the surface or signs of a bad firing job will cause flaking and chipping over time.

Choosing the right equipment is half the challenge; the equally important challenge is to install it correctly. If you're adding these items to an existing bathroom, there's not much you can do in the way of reinforcing them; simply hang them according to the instructions, and hope for the best. If you're doing a gut renovation, however, you have a chance to do something that I do in my own bathrooms. I could literally do a pull-up from my towel rack and not have it pull loose from the wall. And this is the way I've achieved that, for a cost of practically nothing.

When building a bathroom, I either ask the homeowners where they intend to hang their towel bars, or I make a good guess as to where I think they'll go. Then, when the room is framed or stripped down to the framing during a renovation, I take small scraps of lumber, whether 2-by-8s or 2-by-12s, and screw them into the space between the studs. I screw them horizontally into the gap, at about the height of the towel bar or toilet paper dispenser. The wall is then finished with drywall in the ordinary way, and no one knows about the blocking beneath it—that is, until they start to attach the bars. Since they're drilling into the framing rather than into the drywall itself, the result is an extremely solid connection that will not wiggle free of the wall. This blocking will cost all of about $10, and is crucial to a well-built bathroom. Ask your carpenters in advance about this, and if they won't do it—or worse, don't know what you're talking about—then I would advise getting another set of carpenters.

Barring this, there is another way to ensure a solid installation, which can be useful in an existing bathroom where you're not planning to rip apart the walls and add blocking: This is to use a screw called the E-Z Ancor by a company called ITW Buildex. This product comes in metal and plastic, and looks like a corkscrew. You install it in the drywall with a simple Phillips screwdriver. The other end slides through the hardware to screw the towel rack or toilet paper holder into place. While other screws tend to pull out of drywall if they're not firmly anchored into the wood framing of the wall, these sturdy anchors grab tight. They won't wiggle, and are rated for different strengths depending on the size. Most will hold between 35 to 50 pounds, which is more than enough to hold a few damp towels.

A Path of One's Own

A bathroom renovation can be a proving ground for any homeowner's nerves. How could a room that's so small, and so seemingly straightforward, require so much time and effort? And how could it end up costing so much?

An Illuminating Thought

Often considered an afterthought, bathroom lighting ranks as one of the most important considerations in a renovation. You might be able to change the paint color once it's on the walls, but it's far more difficult to alter the positions of light fixtures and mirrors once they are installed.

The key to good lighting lies in the relationship of the lights to the mirror. To make a bathroom mirror effective, the bathroom designers have a golden rule: Illuminate the object that's being reflected—not the reflective surface itself. Never shine a light on the mirror. The best way to create evenly distributed light in front of the bathroom mirror is through a simple concept called cross lighting, where you put fixtures at eye level on either side of the mirror. That way, both halves of your face will be equally well lit without shadows.

By contrast, an overhead light can create weird and unflattering contrasts. If it is shining directly on the top of your head, it will tend to create shadows under your nose, chin, and eyes. This is great for Halloween, perhaps, but not when you're trying to get yourself ready in the morning, or before going out in the evening.

The best approach, I've found, is to use an assortment of lighting types no matter how small the bathroom is. This would include general overhead lighting for quick use of the bathroom, track lighting or wall sconces by the mirror, lighting for over the shower or bathtub, and a similar light near the toilet—especially if the toilet is in a separate compartment. These should each be operated by a separate switch, so you can adjust the lighting as you need it.

Too often, people try to cut corners to get the job done faster and on budget. Sometimes they do this out of ignorance of the systems essential to a long-lasting room; other times, they do it in a misguided attempt to save money. The point is, you can never sacrifice the underlying details that go into a bathroom without paying an even higher price later on. That's because the ultimate test of a successful bathroom renovation lies in its comfort and durability, above anything else. These are important considerations if you're planning on doing the work yourself, but they're just as important to pay attention to if you're hiring someone to do the work for you. Just because you've found a contractor, even a good one, does not mean that every detail will be tended to the way it should. By paying attention to the details in this book, you'll be able to ask the questions—and be willing to pay for the things—that will ensure that the job will get done right.

If you're adventuresome and up for a challenge, go ahead and tackle the project yourself. But first, be sure to educate yourself. Head to a community college for some courses, or a series of courses at the local home improvement center. Above all, consider with care which projects you will do and which ones you should avoid. Plumbing and electrical work, for instance, should never be attempted by a novice with a box of tools. These are professions, after all, and deserve to be treated with respect. If you're hiring a contractor, I have only a few words of advice: A cheap contractor rarely does a good job, but an expensive contractor won't necessarily do a good job, either. To protect yourself, ask for references—a half dozen should do it. Then talk to the satisfied customers on the phone. Ask them how they met the builder (to make sure it isn't their uncle Ed), and how the project worked out. What was the cost overrun? Did the workers arrive when promised? Did everything take place as scheduled, or did the workers disappear for days and weeks on end? Most important, visit one or two of the projects in person, especially if they're similar to what you're planning yourself. Don't regard this as an imposition. The contractor's clients will be more than happy to show off a project they're proud of—as will you, when your own bathroom turns out beautifully. Being choosy up front and being willing to wait for a busy contractor to begin will mean greater happiness in the long run.

Someday soon, when the new bathroom is completed, you'll be able fill up the tub or turn on the shower and take a long, comfortable soak. You've earned it, for a job well done.

Appendix

Being Resourceful
Need more information to plan and renovate a bathroom? Start the search here.

Planning and renovating a bathroom requires a homeowner to be a master of just about everything, from heating and cooling, to electricity, to plumbing, to tiling. And, oh yes, lighting and décor. No single list of resources can ever be complete; if it were, it would be a book in itself. Instead, I've narrowed down the possibilities to include a few that I rely on regularly, and that I know will help get you started. Where they exist, I've included phone numbers, but try the Web sites first. In most cases, you'll find just what you need without having to be put on hold.

ABathroomGuide.Com

www.abathroomguide.com

Billed as "A Homeowner's Guide to Great Bathrooms," this Web site offers useful information and product suggestions on topics such as warm floors, spas, and steam showers.

American Institute of Architects

www.aia.org
1735 New York Avenue, NW
Washington, DC 20006
800-AIA-3837

Use this Web site to find books and design resources, as well as a licensed architect to help turn your bathroom dreams into a workable plan.

American Lighting Association

www.americanlightingassoc.com
P.O. Box 420288
Dallas, TX 75342
800-274-4484

Look on the Web site under "lighting tips and information" for pointers on bathroom lighting; spend $5, and get a booklet on tips for lighting the whole house.

American Society of Interior Designers

www.asid.org
608 Massachusetts Avenue, NE
Washington, DC 20002
202-546-3480

For a list of licensed interior designers in your area start here; also includes tips on how to work with one once you've hired him or her.

Better Homes and Gardens Magazine

www.bhg.com
Meredith Corporation
1716 Locust Street
Des Moines, IA 50309-3023

Search this Web site under "bathroom" to find volumes of information about how to plan a bathroom and choose materials.

DoItYourself.Com

www.doityourself.com

Find answers to bathroom questions on this Web site, including how to use a home equity loan, how to install a fan, and how to tile a tub sur-round.

Hometime.Com

www.hometime.com

The Web site for this popular TV show is a great how-to source for bathroom projects you can tackle yourself—along with a resource guide for books, videos, and manufacturers.

Home Ventilating Institute

www.hvi.org
30 W. University Drive
Arlington Heights, IL 60004
847-394-0150

If ventilation is the topic you're interested in—and it better be if you're renovating a bathroom—this Web site is the one for you. It is filled with detailed information, scientific studies, and product suggestions.

International Association of Lighting Designers

www.iald.org

Suite 9-104

The Merchandise Mart

Chicago, IL 60654

312-527-3677

Designed for the building trade, this Web site contains everything you could possibly want to know about bathroom lighting—as well as tips for working with lighting designers.

Kitchen and Bath Business magazine

www.kitchen-bath.com

VNU eMedia, Inc.

770 Broadway, 6th Floor

New York, NY 10003

This Web site contains a useful question and answer section about bathroom renovation, as well as detailed how-to articles, such as how to tile a floor.

Kitchen and Bath Design News magazine

www.kbdn.net

Cygnus Business Media

1233 Janesville Avenue

Fort Atkinson, WI 53538

Sponsored by a leading magazine for designers, this Web site contains useful tips—such as a primer on glass tiles—as well as buyers' guides for everything in the bathroom.

Marble Institute of America

www.marble-institute.com
28901 Clemens Road, Suite 100
Westlake, OH 44145
440-250-9222

This intriguing Web site offers detailed information on natural stone, including marble, granite, and limestone, and has a resources section with bathroom-oriented topics such as care and cleaning of stone tiles and information on slip resistance.

National Kitchen and Bath Association

www.nkba.org
687 Willow Grove Street
Hackettstown, NJ 07840
877-NKBA-PRO (843-6522)

This comprehensive Web site includes tips from the pros, an ideas section, and a gallery of real bathrooms as well as the stories behind them.

Toiletology.com

www.toiletology.com

This quirky Web site offers a free "course" on repair and maintenance of the toilet with an eye toward saving money and water, with topics such as "How a Toilet Works" and "How to REALLY Clean a Toilet."

Wallcoverings Association

www.wallcoverings.org
401 N. Michigan Avenue
Chicago, IL 60611
312-644-6610

Click on this Web site to learn the basics of wallpapering, including a do-it-yourself guide, information on styles of wallpaper, as well as wallpaper history.

Water Quality Association

www.wqa.org
4151 Naperville Road
Lisle, IL 60532
630-505-0160

To diagnose water problems, head to this Web site, which includes information on contaminants from arsenic to zinc, foul odors, and mineral deposits.

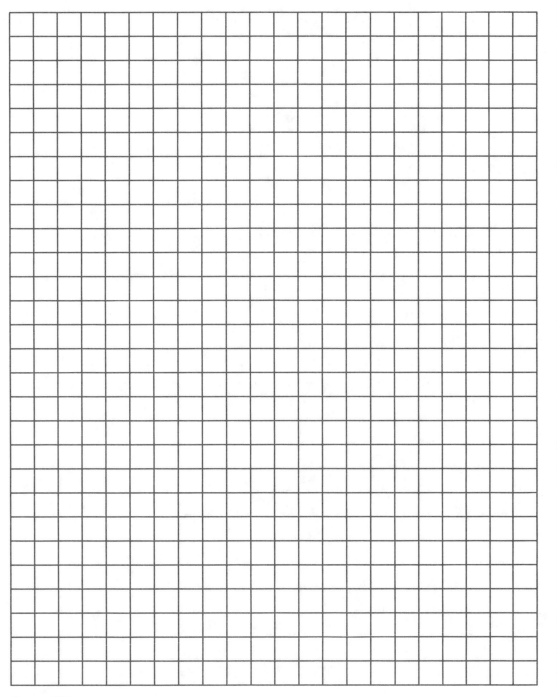

SCALE: 1/4″ TO A FOOT

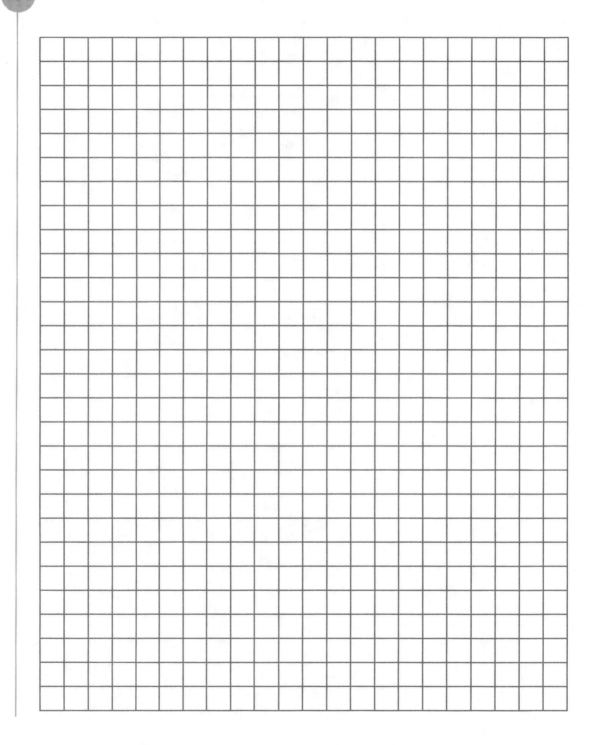

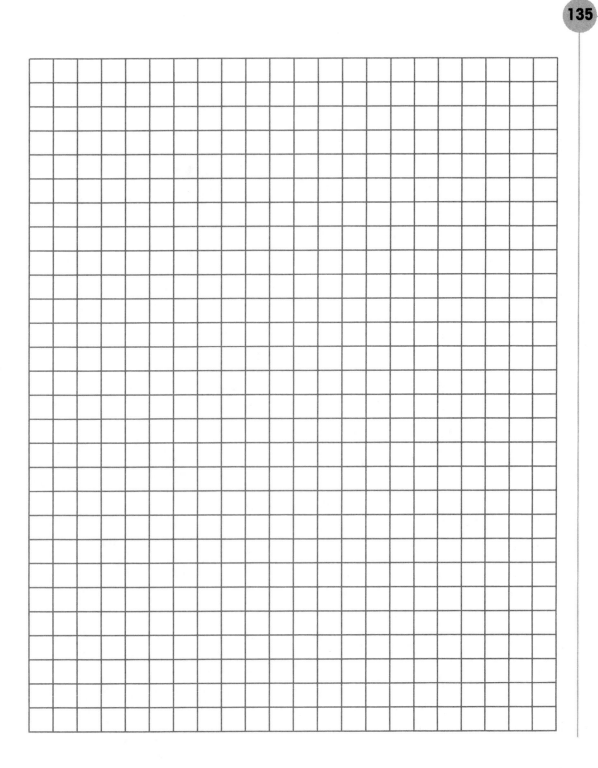

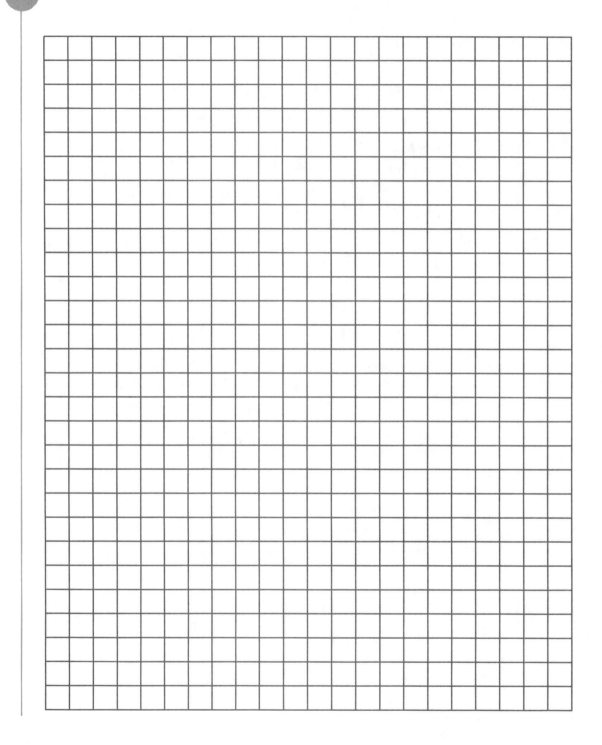

About the Authors

Lou Manfredini started working in a hardware store when he was thirteen years old. He worked as a carpenter's apprentice in college and opened his own construction company in Chicago in 1985. His media career began ten years later when he pitched the idea of a call-in show to a local radio station. WGN-AM picked up the show, and Mr. Fix-It was born. The radio show is now nationally syndicated, and Lou is also a frequent contributor to television and print media, as well. He appears regularly on the *Today Show,* and has a bimonthly column in *USA Weekend.* He still runs his own construction company, and actively builds and renovates homes. Lou lives in Chicago with his wife and four children.

Curtis Rist, an award-winning journalist and author, began his home improvement career a decade ago when he attended house building school, then designed and helped construct his own house. He is a former senior writer at *This Old House* magazine and the coauthor of the *This Old House Homeowner's Manual.* Inspired by working with Lou on their first book, *House Smarts,* he began a new career as a contractor—and now buys and renovates old houses in Hudson, New York, where he lives with his wife and two sons.

Get a better fix on your home-improvement needs with Lou Manfredini's expert advice

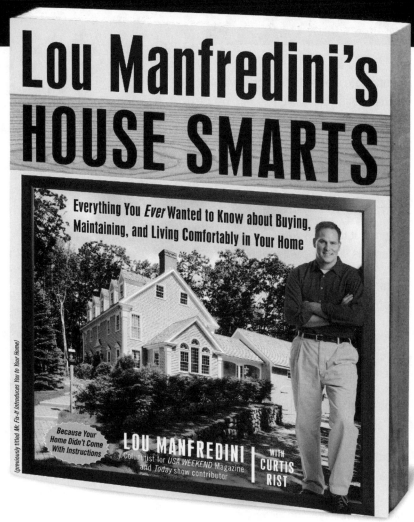

- How an intuitive understanding of your home will help you make the right decisions for its future, as well as your own

- Why it's so important to set your standards high—for yourself, your contractor, and your materials

- The secrets to taming those monsters of the basement: dampness, darkness, concrete floors, and low ceilings

- Why the best way to keep that roof over your head is to know how to maintain it

- The truth behind that most essential and trouble-prone room of the house: the bathroom

- What you've always wanted to know about closets but were afraid to ask

Remember Mr. Fix-It's 3 rules:

Have fun.

Try to be smarter than the materials you're working with.

And...never hold a nail for someone else.

A BALLANTINE BOOKS TRADE PAPERBACK
Available wherever books are sold

Transform a worn-out kitchen into your pride and joy

- Incorporate elements of expensive kitchens into your design

- Tackle intimidating tasks, from new floors to countertops

- Freshen up your cabinets with a dazzling "reface" lift

- Figure out the best ways to bring in natural as well as electric lighting

- Confront issues such as plumbing, color schemes, and layout

- Discover which projects require expert assistance—and which you can handle yourself

- Avoid pitfalls and ask your contractor the right questions

- Improve and add value to your home

Includes illustrations, anecdotes, specific prices, essential tips, and a lifetime of insight

Lou Manfredini's KITCHEN SMARTS

Make over your kitchen with minimum fuss

Save thousands of dollars with handy homebuilders' secrets

Expert advice on "do it yourself" projects

Learn when to get a contractor, and at the lowest cost

LOU MANFREDINI
Columnist for *USA WEEKEND* Magazine and *Today* show contributor
WITH CURTIS RIST

A BALLANTINE BOOKS TRADE PAPERBACK
Available wherever books are sold